BACKSTAGE PASS TO THE FLIPSIDE:

Talking to the Afterlife

with Jennifer Shaffer

Part One

by

Richard Martini

Backstage Pass to the Flipside: Talking to the Afterlife with Jennifer Shaffer Part One by Richard Martini

Copyright © 2018 by Richard Martini. All Rights Reserved.

ISBN: 978-1-7324850-0-6

No part of this book may be reproduced by any mechanical, photographic, or electronic process, other than for "fair use" as brief quotations embodied in articles and review without prior written permission of the author and/or publisher.

The author of this book does not claim the individuals named in this book are the people themselves. There is no way to prove anyone is communicating from the afterlife, nor does author claim doing so.

Also author does not claim to offer medical advice or prescribe the use of any technique as a form of treatment for physical or medical problems without the advice of a physician, either directly or indirectly. The intent of the author is only to offer information of a general nature to help you in your quest for emotional and spiritual well-being. In the event you use any of the information in this book for yourself, which is your constitutional right, the author and the publisher assume no responsibility for your actions.

Homina Publishing PO Box 248 Santa Monica, CA 90406
"Assumption of the Virgin" ("Visions of Paradise") by Francesco Botticcini ("The Palmieri Altarpiece")[1]

---

[1] I chose this artwork before realizing it was commissioned by Matteo Palmieri, forefather of friend Matt; Mary being welcomed "back to the flipside." https://www.florenceinferno.com/botticinis-palmieri-altarpiece-exhibit-london/

CONTENTS

Foreword: Luana Anders and Jennifer Medyln Shaffer

Introduction "A Friend Request"

1 - The Flipside Classroom "A Class in Translation"

2 - Harry Dean Stanton "Open yourself up to the possibility"

3 - Harry Dean Redux "The Concierge of Connectedness"

4 - Interview with Morton "He's Over Your Shoulder"

5 – Morton's Advice "Faster, Smarter, More Efficient"

6 - Harvard to Oxford and Back - Julian Baird PhD

7 - Tom Wilbury "Backstage Pass"

8 - Thanksgiving with The Cowboy Buddha

9 - Robin the Genie "Irony"

10 - Bill from Texas "It's Fun. I Can Fly"

11 - Bill from Texas Part II "I Love Him"

12 – P Rogers Nelson "Surfing the Ethers"

13 – P R Nelson Part II "Don't lose the attachment"

14 - Randal and his friend Harry "It's My Party"

15 – Jennifer Xmas Party "Existential Happiness"

Y.O.U. – A Workbook on How to Talk to the Flipside

Acknowledgements

FOREWORD

by Luana Anders and Jennifer Medlyn Shaffer

My two guides into the Flipside.

Jennifer today and Luana circa 1965.

Forewords are an unusual introduction to the material inside a book. In "Flipside: A Tourist's Guide on How to Navigate the Afterlife" Harvard PhD Gary Schwartz offered to write the foreword, where he said that "self science" was something Einstein had done, and he felt my "journey into the Flipside" should be considered as part of that canon.

In "It's a Wonderful Afterlife volume one" Charles Grodin suggested in his foreword that he didn't quite know what to make of my forays into the afterlife but enjoyed my passion for them. In Volume two, Galen Stoller, a young man who passed away some years ago wrote an eloquent foreword from where he is now, detailing what he wanted to impart about the journey. *"It is a wonderful afterlife,"* he wrote (via a medium), *"but only because "it is wonderful to be alive."*

I suggested my pal and compatriot in this endeavor medium/intuitive Jennifer Shaffer should write the foreword, as she's the conduit for this research. But while we were discussing this, Luana Anders, my friend and inspiration for this journey (who passed in 1996 after our being best friends for 20 years), suggested (through Jennifer) that **she** wanted to write her own foreword to this book.

> *Note: Luana, besides being an actress who appeared in 30 features (including "Easy Rider") also appeared in 300 TV shows. Her film writing credits include "Fire Down Below" and "Limit Up" written with yours truly.) At some point in this book, she suggested I try "automatic writing." I sat in front of the keyboard, put my fingers on the keys and thought; "Type whatever comes to mind." I opened myself up to the possibility I could write something on her behalf:*

"First, let me be clear. Richard is not talking through me. I am talking to him through Jennifer (usually). She does her best to make it easy for him to understand what I'm trying to say, and I'm doing my best to make it easier for him to understand. But it is ***leaning in*** from both sides.

> (Note: Like the 11:11 example Luana cites later in the book.)

At the moment, Richard is typing this sentence and has put his mind on virtual hold (he claims it's a meditation technique) to allow "me" to take over his typing. Some people call this "automatic writing." **Doesn't mean it's any good. It just means it's automatic.** No brain stem involved.

First I'd would like to point out that chanting "Nam Myoho Renge Kyo"[2] saved my life. I know that Richard used to tease me about it, make fun of it – and I'm grateful for that because it allowed me to laugh about it as well.

> (Note: Luana would do her "daimoku" ("Nam-myoho-renge-kyo" prayer) in the car on the way to an event. She'd chant at lightning speed, decades of practice, which sounds a bit like "*homina homina munya homina.*" I would imitate her and she couldn't help but laugh. Chanting helped her navigate her *fear of parties*. Luana was an incredible listener, and on more than one occasion, I'd leave her for ten minutes at some tony event, come back to find a close friend sobbing, pouring out his/her life to her. She had incredible compassion, even as a listener.)

But it saved my life. I never would have made it as long as I did on the planet without being able to focus on something else so dear to me. **Saving humanity by chanting about it.** If you're not familiar with it, if you're suffering, I recommend it as a form of meditation and healing. You pray for someone else and you are healed. Simple as that.

I suggested that I write the foreword to this book because after all, much of it is about me – and I have little to say in the matter. Believe me, it was as shocking to me as it was to my

---

[2] SGI/NSA Buddhist chant. http://www.sgi.org/about-us/president-ikedas-writings/gongyo-and-daimoku.html

class to have him (Richard) appear as he did – willy nilly – in front of my classroom over here.[3]

He just started speaking out loud as if was completely normal that some ghostly avatar would appear in front of our class and start blathering away about his "research."

But I applaud him for it. *He's got cojones this boy.* I can call him a boy – because I know him better than most. He's endearing... to me and to others. But at his core, he's that little boy that I've known for a long, long time.

It's important work that he is doing, important work that he and Jennifer are doing. To help us communicate with all of you back there on the planet, and to open up people's minds about the ability to do so. It's happened not because of any great cataclysmic event that's in the offing – it's happening because *it's time*. **It's time to shift consciousness, to shift gears to understand the nature of reality.**

It's going to upset some people, but we're on top of that as well. It's going to liberate most people. Help most people. And ultimately turn out to be completely accurate when others figure this process out.

Some may ask "Why now?" Some may ask "Is this a good thing to do to communicate with our elders and loved ones who've gone on?" **Well, we still have things to communicate to you, we still have thoughts, dreams,**

---

[3] It was during my first deep hypnosis session where I found myself standing in her classroom, interrupting it. Everyone turned in shock as I appeared. She looked at me as if to say "WTF?" She looked about 20 years younger than when I knew her – at least 10 years before I met her. She looked embarrassed to see me standing in the class talking – but I continued to speak. (*Flipside*)

feelings and hope for humanity – because we consider ourselves part of your journey as well. You may not think of us that way – but we think of you that way.

So please, allow me to offer this small token of appreciation for the fellow who is typing this sentence. Yes, you are a goofball Richard, you are someone that has vexed and frustrated me during my life, but also during other lifetimes.

But you also taught me how to laugh, how to let go, and how to be more of myself while I was on the planet. I know what my path was about, I know why I had to depart early – eventually you'll come to know these reasons as well. Suffice to say it's okay not to "know everything" or "why everything happens" but it is good to trust in the idea that they do "happen for a reason."

And let's focus on that for a moment – "focus on reason." What is reasoning? Taking the evidence presented in front of us, and trying to figure out what it means and how it can help *me* in my journey. We reason things out because that's what we do with our minds... we also can go "beyond reason" and allow things to happen to us, or for us... and that's how I want you to consider what you're about to read. That this goes "beyond reason." And there's a reason for that as well.

Okay, I'm telling Richard to stop now – and to let our mutual friend Jennifer go over this text and see what "resonates" or rings true for her. After all – it's those "feelings of resonance" when we get a shiver of truth, or when we get a feeling that we're actually learning or talking about something that's beyond our logic and thought, beyond our mind... that we truly are able to learn things... about the nature of reality and about the nature of ourselves. I'm fortunate because

Richard can type at the speed of thought – I'm watching him do this as we speak, and I suggest a plethora of ideas and he's able to blast them onto the page.

One more thing about love. **I love you all.** I'm not just saying that as a phrase – but I want you to really feel what I'm saying. I LOVE YOU. I send my heart and soul and unconditional love to you who are reading this sentence. I hope and pray that you receive this love because love is what moves this universe, it is the giant engine of who we are, it's what or who God is, it's what or who *we are*. If you can wrap your mind around love – that's great – if you can't, that's okay too, just open your heart up to the idea of it.

Love yourself. Love your neighbor. Love your enemy. Love the idea of love, of creating love, or spreading love of being loved and giving it in return. That's about all I have to say on the topic except... "See you on the flipside." (To quote a corny phrase too often used by a close friend of both of ours.)

PS: (It's) Just a few days after my birthday – I would have been *xxx* age in your realm – but over here – not such a big deal. Which I prefer. Enjoy the cake.

Written *(as if channeled)* by Luana Anders

Photo of Luana by Tom Pittman circa 1958

Jennifer Shaffer

So, when someone asks me "What does Rich Martini do?" I tell them, **"He can do anything and quickly."** Like he can write a book really fast. Even though in *his* mind it takes *forever*, he can do things that nobody else can do.

I consider him to be, not only a close friend of mine, but a person who has so many great ideas about everything. He knows enough about so many different things to make *this* (what I'm saying about the spirit world) seem tangible. Part of the problem many mediums or intuitives have, is that they have a lot of great ideas, but they can't make them land. Richard makes them land in a great way.

I tell them **"He can take you for a past life adventure like that"** (snaps her fingers). You don't have to lie down or be unconscious for it, it's a state where you are awake, but the information comes through you.

It's just like my work being a medium... I don't remember any of the things that are said to me during my sessions, but I remember feelings associated with it. I feel like I'm in a dream state. And you know how when you wake up from a dream, you think you're going to remember it? But you don't. (Laughs) That's basically my whole day at work.

It's something he can do while you're fully conscious. **He asks questions that nobody else asks, that's why he's such a great interviewer. He gets to the core of things that you didn't even know existed.**

And for people that are afraid of this kind of investigation, Richard has a way of just making them open up; whether they want to or not. He has a great way of bringing forth what's bothering you or hurting you to the surface. I've had situations where I've often looked to him for guidance.

I think he is like a therapist for mediums, and he does it in a way that is non-threatening. You may not remember the things that happened in a previous lifetime, but your energy field does. And by examining what may have happened your energy field slowly but surely starts healing; not just from this lifetime but from all different lifetimes.

In terms of what it is we're doing: I was talking to someone this morning. When I get direct information, sometime I don't say it the way that I hear it, because I don't want to offend them. This woman came through, and said, "Tell my daughter the reason she is a good mother is because I was not a good mother."

But I was trying to sugar coat for her and her mother came through and said "Stop sugar coating it! Tell her exactly what I'm trying to say! I was NOT a good mother and that's why she IS an incredible mother." The mother was grateful that she lived *her* life so that she could be an example to help her daughter become a better mother. The daughter started crying, saying "You're right."

Speaking the truth doesn't mean you can't be loving or kind; but you must stop sugar coating the truth. When I report what I'm seeing or sensing, I often think "What if I'm wrong?" But when someone says blatantly "Stop sugar coating it. Tell her I was a horrible mother and she's going to understand it" – I have to repeat what I'm hearing. As it turns out, that comment meant more to her than anything. So that's one thing I try to do; it's not my job to prove to anyone that I'm speaking to the afterlife, but it is my job to speak truthfully about what I'm getting.

Rich: In that vein, a film studio friend told me he thought what we were doing had to be either "imaginary" or "coincidence." I was reminded of a story he once told me; he was meeting the new head of the studio and was asked "How many movies do we make a year that fail?" My friend answered, "Statistically, about half." And the new studio head said "Well, let's just not make the ones that fail."

I try to focus on the examples where we get positive results and try to understand how that can occur. For me, it's important to ask, "What is the mechanism that allowed Jennifer to get new information from the Flipside that turned out to be true?" And "how could she casually refer to something that only I could possibly know?" In that sense this investigation helps those on the flipside to better communicate with their loved ones back here.

So in this book there's not going to be any sugar coating. But "Caveat Emptor;" buyer *"be aware*:" If this book is going to disturb you in any way, please, give it back, get a refund. *"These are not the droids you're looking for."* We aren't here to change your paradigm or prove anything to anyone.

But for those of you who do stick around, I want to remind you; *"All roads lead to home."* It doesn't matter what your background is, what your beliefs have been; what you are about to hear is verbatim from people who are "back home" – (the term they use to mean *no longer here.)* We're going to help those folks "back home" to stay in touch, stay connected with those who are *not yet* back home.

But buckle up; it's going to be a bumpy ride.

Luana and author on Via Veneto.

When I put this photo on the fridge I said aloud *"Well, that's the essence of our relationship."* (Drinking cappuccinos and eating cookies.)

After she passed, we invited medium James Van Praagh to appear on our mutual friend Charles Grodin's talk show.

Secretly, Charles arranged for me to call in and see if we could "speak" to Luana. On air, James said, "She's saying to tell Richard there's a photograph on his refrigerator that she says is "The essence of your relationship."

It was the first time I realized it was physically possible to still talk to her. Recently, while discussing her foreword and how she helped me write it, she gave Jennifer the image of Tinkerbell, said to her "I sat over his shoulder and whispered it into his ear. He should look at page 13, at the end of that chapter, for verification." (This message was before I'd shown the book to anyone.)

Notice what page the foreword ends.

The following is a continuation of that conversation.

INTRODUCTION

"A FRIEND REQUEST"

Jennifer and Richard in our usual cafe.

It all began with a *"friend request"* on Facebook.

It was from someone I didn't know, had never met. "Hmm. Who's this?" I thought. When I clicked *"accept"* she replied with a clip of holding up her cell phone to a cheering crowd of friends saying, *"Rich Martini accepted my friend request!"*

I thought that was pretty funny and assumed she must have mistaken me for someone else entirely.

Jennifer assured me she was a fan of my books "Flipside" and "It's a Wonderful Afterlife" and told me that during her recent Thanksgiving festivities, the audible version of my books played in her headset while she was doing the dishes. She said she felt as if I was "speaking directly to her."

She told me she was an intuitive/medium and that she worked in nearby Manhattan Beach. "Maybe we can have coffee or lunch sometime," she said.

I told her that I had not focused on mediumship in my research about the flipside for a couple of reasons. 1. People go to mediums, generally, to learn their future. My research shows that the future is not set but there are "likely outcomes." And 2, people tend to see mediums for advice about their love life. *"Will I be with this person in the future?"* Well, if you understand the architecture of the flipside, you've probably already been with them before, likely will be with them again, and even if they run off with someone else, you can address that at a later date with them when "you're back home." And besides, like Jennifer, already happily married.

But then I realized, *wait a second,* I had spoken to a couple of mediums in the past who had claimed to be in contact with a famous individual on the flipside.

I was working on the film "Salt" in Manhattan, and a close friend introduced me to Pattie Canova, a tough smart medium who grew up on the streets of Manhattan. I helped Pattie with some advice about a script she wrote; she said, "Let me do a reading for you as a return favor."

I said, "No, thanks, *"you're preaching to the choir."* She insisted. She laid out some playing cards and said "You're working on a film about a pilot. A female pilot. Amelia Earhart?" I looked at my friend as if she had set me up for a laugh. She had not. I had been working on a script about Amelia Earhart for around 20 years at this point.

I thought – "Well, why am I resisting this?" If she can "speak to Amelia" maybe I can clear up some issues about her story. So, I spent two hours interviewing someone who knew more about Amelia than anyone I had ever encountered in my years of research. I pursued this new information and her new leads until I ran into another medium. That was through Dr. Elisa Medhus, a Houston doctor whose son had died, and had "called her on the phone" from the flipside.[4]

Elisa wrote about her son's passing, and what he told her about the flipside and later, with the help of medium Jamie Butler, her son Erik wrote a book about his journey ("My Life After Death"). I began conversing with Dr. Medhus about her method of "interviewing people in the afterlife" with her son's help. I casually said, "You should interview Amelia Earhart sometime." She said, "She's scheduled for an interview on Tuesday." *(What are the odds?)*

I asked to see the questions she was asking the famed aviatrix, mostly culled from Wikipedia and "common knowledge" about her journey. I asked if I could supply the questions and amended hers to reflect what I knew about Amelia.

For example, I had the medium (Jamie Butler) ask "Who was the love of your life, and was it a painter?" Now in this construct – Jamie is sitting in front of the camera and is seeing "Erik Medhus" on the flipside, who brings forth various people to be interviewed. In this case, the medium Jamie said she saw both Amelia and what appeared to be her husband George Putnam standing behind her.

Jamie confirmed to me later that she didn't know anything about Amelia's life, that she doesn't prepare for these interviews, but just reports what she "sees."

The answer Amelia gave to my question was "I think my life has been a good example to young girls everywhere, and I'm

---

[4] ChannelingErik.com

not really interested in changing people's opinions about my journey, but yes, the love of my life was a woman, and she was indeed a painter."

How did I know that? Because I worked on her life for 20 years, I'm credited for research on both Diane Keaton and Hilary Swank's film versions or her story. I knew she had an open marriage, found out through interviews that Dorothy Putnam (George's wife) had walked in on her husband with two other women in his bed (one was Amelia) prior to their divorce. (Their divorce was amicable, mutual, as Dorothy married her boyfriend the following weekend in Vegas.)

Dr. Medhus asked my questions, including what really happened to her after she disappeared (Amelia landed the Electra on Mili atoll, which I already knew and have filmed eyewitnesses about) and learned that indeed she was incarcerated (arrested by the Japanese and taken to their Military Headquarters in Saipan) and how she died of dysentery on Saipan just prior to the Americans arrived in 1944 when they found her plane and her briefcase.[5]

As it turns out, Pattie Canova had told me roughly the same story I was now hearing from Jamie Butler (even though I wasn't present, Dr. Medhus filmed the session and sent me a copy.) And at the end of the interview, "Amelia" said something to Jamie that I did not hear until I transcribed the audio two years after it was made.

Jamie asked, "So how did you die? Were you shot or beheaded?" (At that point, I'd heard both.) Amelia didn't respond for some time, then said "I'm not comfortable

---

[5] Covered extensively at the website EarhartOnSaipan.com

discussing that in this public form, but if the person **who wrote the questions** wants to speak to me privately, I will tell him."

At the time, when I heard it, my skeptical mind thought that was the medium saying, "But if the guy who crafted these questions wants to do a private reading with me, I'll help him." It wasn't until I transcribed it, I realized Amelia was speaking directly to me. *Cause I'm the guy who crafted the questions.*

This all flashed through my head as I was speaking to Jennifer on the phone. I said, "What kind of mediumship do you do?" She said, "Well, I work with law enforcement agencies nationwide to help with missing person cases."

I said, "How'd you like to work on the most famous missing person case in history?" She said, "I'm in, whoever it is."

So, when I went to meet her, I brought my camera, and filmed a three-hour interview with her and Amelia Earhart, George Putnam and whoever else wanted to swing by and put in their two cents. She confirmed precisely what I had learned in 20 years of research, and said the same answers that the other two mediums had told me – I asked roughly the same 20 questions to all three mediums, and all three replied with information that is not known to the public, including new information about what happened to her.

Got that?

It was new information about Amelia from people who could not possibly know the information. Information that confirmed my decades of research, but also new information that I've been able to subsequently research and verify. (Or in the case of "where her plane is," the next time I get to Saipan, I'll dig it up.)

This story for the most part is covered in *"Hacking the Afterlife."* I won't be discussing that part of it here, except that indeed, Miss Earhart shows up in our "group talks" in this book, and still has a thing or two to say about her life story. (So, she will be referenced from time to time.)

What made my interview with Jennifer so amazing, was that while we were discussing "What happened to Amelia's body?" Jennifer said, "She's showing me that when the two soldiers dug up her body, they only found an arm."

Not everyone is aware that two GI's claim they dug up her body on Saipan (Fred Goerner, CBS correspondent wrote about them in his book *"Searching for Amelia"* but it's not common knowledge), and I was startled to hear Amelia say there were "two GI's" – something that Jennifer did not know. But further there was **"new information"** in what she said.

In Goerner's book, there's no mention of what they found. Just that they had been ordered to dig her up, and in the second edition of his book, he interviewed both GI's who confirmed that indeed they had gone out into the jungle and dug up two bodies and were told one of them was Amelia's. But nothing about an arm.

Ten minutes after my filming Jennifer, I got a call from Jim Hayton, an NTSB expert who lives in Seattle. He's been on the forefront (with his friend Dick Spink) of verifying pieces of her Electra that Dick Spink found on Mili Atoll. (They were featured in the History Channel episode about her.) Jim was calling because he had just seen documentation from another researcher that "proved everything I had told him about Amelia." Jim said, "Rich, that story about those two GI's who dug up Amelia's body was in the research, but it says something different; "they only recovered her arm."

I gasped. I had just heard the same obscure detail "from Amelia herself." *What are the odds?* The exact same sentence said ten minutes earlier about these GI's only finding her arm. I've subsequently found an interview with those two GI's (from the Chicago Tribune 1977) where they said they "only recovered an arm and a partial rib cage." Which verifies what Jennifer had told me, corroborates what Jim had told me, and was a "new piece of information" that came to me direct from the flipside.

But again, this introduction isn't about Amelia.

One day I hope to make that film about her, I've reported this information on my website "EarhartOnSaipan.com" and in the book *"Hacking the Afterlife"* – But I'm here to introduce to you, ladies and gentlemen, the one and only Jennifer Shaffer.

Since that first meeting, we've been getting together a couple of times a month. I bring my camera along with me, we have lunch somewhere and I film our chats about the flipside. I may ask her to "bring someone forward" or she may announce "so and so is here." I am not trying to prove that person is "here" – because as you've just heard, she's already proven her accuracy to me on many occasions.

She's the first person to observe that what she sees or hears is subject to interpretation. She may see a metaphor, or hear a turn of a phrase, and then tries to explain what she thinks they mean. Folks on the flipside generally don't "speak" – they show an image, sometimes impart a feeling. So communicating directly to the flipside, to loved ones no longer on the planet, is not a "dial up" kind of process.

It depends how good *they* are at communicating (apparently it takes some learning and getting used to) – if you can imagine a jet plane slowing down to drive alongside of a Volkswagen van and communicating with the passengers while the windows are rolled up... it's an apt metaphor. Or think of a person standing outside the fish tank and tapping on the glass, and we, *the little fish,* come to the edge of the tank and stare at them as they try to speak slowly and loudly to us. It's not an easy task.

But we'll get into all that.

We're going to show how easy it is to speak to people on the flipside and gain new information from them. It won't be information that will harm your own path or journey in any way, but it will be enough verifiable information so that you realize "There's more than meets the eye" with regard to reality.

Jennifer works with law enforcement agencies nationwide to help with cases, including "missing person" events. I've met some of the parents whose lives she's healed with her work. I'm aware of a few cases she's solved using her abilities, and know why they seek her help. She's an excellent reporter of what she feels or senses.

Let's chat about the process for a moment; I liken what we do to stringing up paper cups as we did in our youth. Jennifer is my Dixie cup connection to the afterlife. She's my cellphone to those who no longer on the planet. My friend Howard Schultz (creator of "Extreme Makeover" and other TV shows) did a between life session with Scott De Tamble[6] (it was in the book "Flipside" - "River of Souls.") Scott helped him chat with his mother, who had crossed over. Howard said his mom explained how "talking to her" was equivalent to picking up a cellphone.

She said "You push buttons, don't know how the process works, but when we answer you know it's a loved one on the line. When you think or pray to us, we can hear you – we might not be able to answer you right away but if we can respond to you, we will."

Howard passed away a couple of years after that filmed session. Happy to report that Howard has made a number of appearances at our lunches. He continues to be an active source of comedy from the flipside.

I film and transcribe our sessions; the interviews have been edited for clarity and time and sometimes "to protect someone still on the planet." Although they tend to have very little discretion when telling Jennifer something about their path, neither of us want to embarrass anyone still working their way through their journey. Grief and grieving are key to our development as souls; we must allow that "hearing someone is still accessible" could be disconcerting to some folks.

But by and large, by "opening ourselves up to the possibility" that there is an afterlife is a therapeutic method of healing. I got that turn of phrase from Harry Dean Stanton, after he crossed over, as you'll see in an ensuing chapter. **"Allow for**

---

[6] www.lightbetweenlives.com

the possibility that there is an afterlife" – and that goes a long way to relieving stress for many people.

Finally, a word about *"celebrity."*

As reported in "Flipside" I heard a phrase in Latin during a dream; *"Vanum populatum."* I learned during my between life session (conducted by Jimmy Quast, trained by Michael Newton)[7] that the phrase was said to me by my "higher self" in order to get me to look it up in the dictionary and contemplate it's meaning.

It means *"annihilate vanity."* (My answer; "I live in LA, where do I begin?") But since then, I see vanity, celebrity as icing of the cake of who we are – fame, fashion, money, ego are all extensions of that concept. "What someone looks like, what kind of car they drive, none of that's important..." (I just remembered I wrote that dialog in a scene for *"You Can't Hurry Love"* which the character Eddie Hayes says directly into camera. I was annihilating vanity even when I wasn't aware that it was something I was doing back in the 1980's.)

But when someone "famous" shows up at our classroom, I ascribe that to Luana. As noted, she was in 30 feature films (from Dementia 13, to Easy Rider, to the Godfather) over 300 TV shows, was friends with many icons in her field including Charles Grodin, Paul Simon, Art Garfunkel, Robert Towne and Jack Nicholson.[8] I've had several friends claim that she "appeared" to them in a dream with specific messages for them. (Even from friends who "never met her.") They claim

---

[7] eastonhypnosis.com

[8] LuanaAnders.com

her words of wisdom "helped them" navigate some issue in their lives. *So that's a bit unusual.*

Recently, my wife Sherry said Luana visited her in a dream. Sherry asked her "But how can you be here? You died over 20 years ago." Luana jokingly showed her a toy "rocket ship" as if that was her mode of transport. But then she showed Sherry an image of "11:11." She said. "You're on one side, and I'm on the other side, and we meet at the decimals."

Sherry didn't understand the comment but I feel I do. If you think as 11 as a hallway on this side (like an architect's drawing or blueprint) and the other a hallway on the Flipside – she's saying, "we both need to adjust our frequency in order to meet in the middle where the decimals are."

11:11.

Which is basically what this book is about. Adjusting your frequency so you can communicate directly with your loved ones who are no longer on the planet. Not gone, just not here. To figure out how to gain your own "backstage pass" to the flipside.

This book is not about *celebrity*, not about *talking to celebrities.* As noted, the people who show up are people that I knew, Jennifer knew, or who knew or met Luana. The idea is, if there's a frequency we are familiar with, or Luana is familiar with, they have an easier time of showing up "in our class." It's short hand to ask for someone that we all know to come forward and speak to us – whether it's Bill Paxton or Harry Dean Stanton. They are celebrities to some, but old acquaintances of mine (as we'll learn.)

And finally, a word about mistakes and errata. I noticed recently that somehow my computer would open a copy of my screenplay about Amelia Earhart. I asked Jennifer about it – she said, "Amelia did that, to remind you to stay engaged to a film about her." But back home, my daughter admitted she "clicked on the icon that brought up the script by accident about once a month."

So, there you have it! Proof that the afterlife does not exist! *Amelia was wrong!* It was my daughter accidentally hitting the same button... but then *in my head,* I heard, "Yeah, but who do you think gets her to click on that button?" D'oh! Foiled again by **the voice in my head.**

In that vein; please take this research with as much salt as required. Jennifer *may be* talking to people on the Flipside, we may be talking to *versions of people* on the flipside, we may be *"meddling with the primal forces of nature"* (a quote from the film "Network.")

I wrote music reviews for Variety in the 1990's, a gig offered me by my dear friend, music editor and bandmate Bruce Haring (Variety, Billboard). Bruce and I would sometimes travel together to music festivals and there was always a *meshegas* of obtaining the right pass for the right venue. We had run into our mutual pal Edna Gundersen, the then music critic of USA Today who was wearing a particular colored pass. When the promoters handed over our passes, I noticed they were a "lesser color" than hers. I said, "Excuse me, we'd like the same color pass that Edna has." He scoffed. "You mean an "All Access Backstage Pass?" Sorry. *Edna is Edna."*

Well, we do have access to the backstage, and we're going to grant you, dear reader, an "All access backstage pass" to the flipside.

But first, let's ask the "bouncer" that protects your subconscious from these flights of fancy to take a step back from the velvet rope guarding your mind so we can all go into this Afterlife Club together.

Join us on the other side of the velvet rope, won't you?

*****

Luana is tapping her wrist; class is waiting.

CHAPTER ONE:
OUR FLIPSIDE CLASSROOM
"A Class in Translation"

Including visits from Chris Cornell, David Bowie with assistance from "classmates" Prince and Robin Williams.

Class moderator Luana Anders circa 1965

While Jennifer and I had been meeting regularly to "talk to whomever showed up" this is the first session where the idea of a *Flipside classroom* came up.

For those unfamiliar with the concept, I initially heard about "classrooms in the afterlife" from my friend Luana. As she was dying, one day she said, "I think when I die, I'm going to another galaxy." We had never talked about death openly – it was just a topic neither of us would discuss. But in this instance, she opened the door for me to ask, **"Why do you think that?"**

She told me she had a recurring dream where she was in a classroom, everyone was "dressed in white" and speaking a language "She'd never heard before, but somehow completely understood." I thought *"Oh, that must be from the morphine drip"* (that she had helping ease her pain from cancer.) But the day she passed her close friend Sandra Stephenson called me from Hawaii and said "I had the most wonderful dream about her last night. She was in the 4th dimension, and she was in a spiritual classroom where everyone was dressed in white."

I asked the hospice nurse Charmaine about it, and she nearly fainted. **"That was her recurring dream!"**

I moved to New York City to work on the Charles Grodin show with her good friend Charles, and while there I had an out of body experience where I felt I went to see her. It was fairly dramatic, as I've had the experience of "floating around the room" in the past, but in this case, it was like a "blast off" where I left my bed in the upper west side of Manhattan, shot into deep space, tumbled through a worm hole or black hole, and found myself traveling with great speed to suddenly screech to a halt; Luana standing in front of me.

It was Luana as I knew her – but with her eyes closed. She opened them as if to say **"You were wondering where I am. This is where I am."**

At that moment, a truck driver hit his horn – but I had the experience of "traveling back" to New York, like the Charles

Eames film *"Powers of Ten"*[9] – hurtling through deep space, back to Manhattan from above to suddenly sitting up in my bed – all before the driver took his hand off the horn.

It was as if she was saying **"Not only do I still exist, but this is where you can find me."** I thought, **"Well, if she still exists somewhere off planet, or off universe, and she can come and visit me, how can I go and visit her?"**

Some years later, when I began to research the topic of the Flipside, I found an account in Michael Newton's book *"Journey of Souls"* where the person under deep hypnosis said, "I see myself in a classroom and everyone is dressed in white." I chill went up my spine and I knew if I was looking for Luana, this would be a method of how to find her.

The first time I did a between life session, I went to visit *two* classrooms. (Hypnotherapist said, "Where would you like to go?" I said, "To find my friends.") The first classroom was fun, welcoming – the teacher seemed to know me well and introduced me to her young students. I did not consciously recognize this "teacher" but she seemed to know me and praised me to her class, who all were "turned in their seats" in my direction, as if to say *"Oh, teacher's friend is here!"*

However, I later said, "I want to visit Luana's class," when I arrived, I had the impression I was interrupting her class, mid lecture. It was the polar opposite of the journey to the first class.

Imagine yourself sitting in a room with fellow students and suddenly this hologram appears saying *"Okay, I'm here visiting a class in the afterlife!"* The students all turned to

---

[9] https://youtu.be/0fKBhvDjuy0 "Powers of 10" by Charles Eames

look at me, as if they were not used to interruptions. The teacher stopped his lecture and everyone went silent. I shut up for a few seconds, and then said, *"I get the feeling I'm not supposed to be here, but since I've come all this way, I might as well continue."*

I saw Luana sitting in the back of the classroom looking at me as if saying *"What the hell? What are you doing here?"* and I explained (to the hypnotherapist, knowing I was filming this session) that this was a class in *"Accessing the healing light of the universe, and these students learn how to help healers, doctors and others to connect to that energy to heal people on Earth."*

At which point one student turned in his desk and mockingly said, *"You don't know what the hell you're talking about."*

I was startled; obviously I was interrupting them and not welcome. I said to the hypnotherapist **"Okay, a student just turned and corrected me. What I meant to say is that people in this class learn how to help doctors and healers to access the "healing light of the universe," however not all people sign up for a lifetime where they will heal everyone, and likewise people may sign up for a lifetime to experience an illness, so they can learn from it."**

To which the student said **"Well, I guess you do know something after all."**

A very weird exchange. My conscious mind was thinking "If I'm making this up, why am I making up this unhappy student challenging me? If I'm not supposed to be here, then have I broken some cardinal rule by coming here?" It was so foreign to me that when the session was over, I literally felt as if the axis of the Earth had shifted slightly – like "everything I thought I knew" had to be rethought.

Two years later with a different hypnotherapist (first was with Jimmy Quast, the second with Scott De Tamble[10]) I decided to "revisit" the classroom, not knowing if I could be able to return there. (I.e., "what if it was all a fantasy I had created?" and the second "between life journey" sent me elsewhere?)

But after a few seconds of Scott De Tamble "walking me down a stairway of time" *("You're getting younger now")* I interrupted him to say, "I'm already back there." It felt as if the garden gate had been left open, and it was like walking back to where I had left off two years before.

When I "arrived" back in Luana's classroom, it was as if *only twenty minutes* had gone by, even though it was physically two years after my first "visit." I was aware I was now standing in front of this huge classroom, Luana apologizing to her teacher for my rude behavior (from two years earlier but felt like twenty minutes earlier) trying to explain what it was that I was doing. After her explanation the teacher turned to me. **"So, what did you want to know?"**

So, I'm familiar with the concept of "seeing a class" on the flipside. In this following session with Jennifer, it was the day after the musician Chris Cornell had apparently committed suicide. When someone "shows up" in a session and claims to be Chris Cornell, or David Bowie or someone else that neither Jennifer and I have met, I report what they say and try to search the facts to see what might be accurate.

---

[10] Jimmy Quast EastonHypnosis.com Scott De Tamble LightBetweenLives.com

My questions are in *italics*, Jennifer's answers are in normal type face, **answers she's getting are in bold type**.

*****

Rich: I thought we'd see if we can access someone neither one of us knows. We're going to try and dial up Chris Cornell. Let's ask Luana if she can dial him up?

Jennifer: Luana just goes and grabs him.

Rich: Oh! That was easy. Chris did a sublime cover of Prince's song "Nothing Compares to U" and since we've had Prince show up in our conversations before, I thought maybe they might have known each other. Chris? Say hello to the guy who wrote this song.

> (Note: Prince, or someone who appears as Prince Rogers Nelson is a frequent visitor to our class, as we'll see in ensuing chapters. He appears in *"Hacking the Afterlife"* as well.)

Jennifer: I just got chills.

Rich: Well, if anyone can talk to him that we know, it would be The Purple One. Can you help be a conduit for us?

They said, "Yes." I keep getting Robin Williams. Some group they're dealing with?

Robin was awarded a "Comedy Chair" today at USC.

Jennifer applauds.

Who wants to help us talk to Chris?

They're like dragging him over, he's hands are out like, "No, I don't wanna go on camera!" They're all laughing.

Can we ask you questions?

"Yes." (Jennifer aside) It's funny; I was going to talk to Chris tonight for a radio call in show.

> (Note: Jennifer does a number of shows where people ask her direct questions about people on the flipside.)[11]

Think of this as a preshow for Chris. What does he look like to you?

He has his hair back.

Can Prince and Robin help us with him? Perhaps their presence would give us credibility with Chris.

Luana just said "Don't forget me" and that guy... the one who had the song "Don't you forget about me" in his film.

John Hughes?

Yeah.

> (Note: John Hughes came through during a session previously. I had met him on the set of *"Pretty in Pink"* and he went to my high school. He had some specific messages for friends that know him, including his wife Nancy. Nancy and John eloped in high school, the same high school depicted as Shermer High in "Ferris Bueller.")

Rich: Well, what about John? Is he accessible?

---

[11] For an account of Chris Cornell's last days: https://www.rollingstone.com/music/features/chris-cornell-david-fricke-on-soundgarden-singer-final-days-w484560)

Jennifer: He's showing me a huge tombstone.

That's correct. He has one in the cemetery in Lake Forest, a gorgeous piece of cut marble with only his last name on it.

(Jennifer, to me:) **Do you have a sister? He says he's in love with your sister.**

I don't have a sister, but I know who he's talking about. One of my sisters-in-law was his close pal, she and my niece were hanging out with John and his family the day he passed in Manhattan. He went to the same high school as I did.

He says both he and his wife loved your sister-in-law. They were very close.

> (Note: *(ding!)* This is one of those **"bells of verification."** Jennifer could not know that my brother and his wife were pals with John, or that my sister-in-law was a light in both his and his wife's lives or that John had known my sister-in-law since high school.)

Does he have any message for his widow?

He's showing me an image of her running. He says, "Tell her "Don't run from your feelings."

What's that mean?

He says "Tell her to not run from her feelings. She likes someone. She's afraid to show it."

Well, I think both my sister-in-law and John's wife are skeptics about talking to the flipside. What could I tell his family that only they would know about him?

He's showing me that he had a previous heart attack. One just prior to the big one, like a few hours and then another one six years earlier. He said, "She'll know about that one."

Okay. Hey, whatever happened to the copy of "Limit Up" that I gave you?

> (Note: I sent a copy of my film "Limit Up" with Ray Charles to John in hopes of working for him someday. I try to keep these conversations light so that it's not only about the loss of an individual, but minor details help us verify it's really them we're talking to.)

He showed me an image of it being tossed into a box. It was VHS, right?

*Yes, it was. (**ding!**) I accidentally left the note from Oliver Stone telling me he enjoyed the film in the VHS copy.*

He's showing me that he wasn't well at the time. Sweating, out of breath; heart issues. He was in no space to look at it at the time. He says, "Tell your sister-in-law not to hold back."

What does that mean?

He said, "No one has ever come over from that side to this side saying, "Gee I wish I had held back more during my life." Don't hold back."

> (Note: I think this observation is worth repeating. **"No one ever comes over to the flipside wishing that they held back more during their lifetime."** It's such a smart thing to observe, and contrary to anything Jennifer or I have been raised to believe

about the afterlife. But it is repeated in the research. *You're here on the planet to live, love, have fun. Don't forget to have fun!*)

Jennifer: Oh, Robin (Williams) is bringing forth John Candy. They're both saying, "We need to bring back Old Hollywood."

Rich: And of course, John Candy, one of the all time greats, thank you very joining us.[12]

It's like they are all sitting in a classroom.

Are they in rows?

They keep coming up one by one, they showed me it's a classroom. Luana is in charge of this classroom – not in a hierarchy way, but in a moderator way.

What are they learning in this class?

"Translation."

It's a class in translation of the ethers in some way?

"Yes." Someone else just came in.

I'm sorry, who just came in?

The airplane girl.

Oh, Amelia. Are you part of this class or are you just sitting in?

---

[12] I did see John Candy perform with Second City in Chicago, while the Toronto company switched. I met him in a bar on La Cienega in LA, and got everyone in the place to give him a standing ovation. He was flattered and laughed about it.

She says, "She's helping them too."

> (Note: As noted above, I had asked three different mediums the same questions to Amelia Earhart, whose story I've been working on for three decades. Each one got the same answers. When Jennifer came into my life, I took the opportunity to "interview Amelia" extensively, to confirm or deny what 30 years of research had shown me.)[13]

Okay, so this is a class in communication, is that correct?

"Yes, they're telling me about the future, and how this form of communication will grow over time."

(Trying to stay on track) Guys, we're here to talk to Chris. We don't care about the future.

They said *"bullshit!"* They all laughed.

I hate to herd cats, but we've got a few folks to talk to here today. The question at hand; Chris did you check yourself out? And if you're aware of it, "Why?"

He showed me his blood stream, an imbalance. He said it was regarding a break up, "but not the way you think." There was a possible divorce... it wasn't public knowledge... He's saying that on a certain level he knew he was checking out.

Was it like an "exit point?"

---

[13] As recounted in "Hacking the Afterlife." Createspace publishing 2016. https://www.goodreads.com/book/show/31280554-hacking-the-afterlife

(Note: As we'll hear, "exit points" are short hand for a moment when people might have left the planet, but did not for whatever reason, or in this case, chose to "take an exit." I have no way of knowing if there was a break up involved, but am reporting verbatim what she's saying.)

I asked about the method of his passing, and Robin jumped up and made a face. *"Drugs!"* **he said.**

Class! Behave.

They're making fun of us. Hold on; Chris is talking. He showed me 5 pm last night. I feel like he just didn't think he would survive... He's showing me veins.[14]

I know he had a drug problem before... Chris what was your experience like crossing over to the flipside?

Wow. He says "Music. Beautiful music." He said, "At first he was scared."

What was the music? Classical, ethereal? Rock and roll?

Music he's never heard from before. But the first person he saw was Prince. And then David Bowie.

---

[14] His wife reported, "I noticed he was slurring his words; he was different," she said in a statement issued May 19th. "When he told me he may have taken an extra Ativan or two, I contacted security and asked that they check on him." Soundgarden bodyguard Martin Kirsten kicked in the hotel-room and bedroom doors – both were locked – and found Cornell "with blood running from his mouth and a red exercise band around [his] neck," according to a police report. https://www.rollingstone.com/music/news/chris-cornells-wife-issues-statement-w483179

(Note: This will sound odd to anyone just picking up this book. You'll see that "I was met by a friend I know" is common in many of these reports. It's in line with what people say under deep hypnosis about remembering what happened after a death in a previous lifetime, it's consistent with reports of people who claim to have met people during a near death event (NDE).

We are often met by our loved ones, but as we're going to find out in this book, "friends show up" to give us a "soft landing" by calming us with their presence. (Their words.) David Bowie was known to Chris, so seeing him would be "someone *he* knew." Also "showing his veins" doesn't necessarily mean he was shooting drugs (He told his wife he'd taken some Ativan) but could mean a general example of "this has been going on for awhile.")

Chris, did you know David?

He met him a long time ago, at a benefit, I guess. (Jennifer; aside) I've never seen David Bowie before.

(Note: This is worth noting; *(ding!)* Jennifer would have no clue that Chris had met Bowie. Chris met David at a Vanity Fair photoshoot in 2001 celebrating their November "Music" issue and posted about it after Bowie passed: "I was part of a Vanity Fair music issue, where there were a lot of pretty amazing people there for a photo shoot. He (Bowie) was one of them... he saw **I was uncomfortable and went out of his way to alleviate that discomfort and make me**

feel happy about it. It was a compassionate moment.")[15]

Well, can we talk to you for a second, David? What was it like for you crossing over? Who was there to greet you and what did you feel?

He showed me the music video he made.

"Black Star?" (David Bowie's last music video which was about crossing over to the flipside.) Was that what the experience was like?

He's laughing. He said it (the video) was a **"100th of that, of what it really was, and it was related to the kind of beauty that can't be expressed, or colors that can't be expressed through this dimension, so many lights of all the people he's known or felt."** He says that his father... his father was the first one that came forward.[16]

Okay.

He's showing me a letter... a love letter to his wife... I don't know if he wrote it before he left or if he hid it. (Pause) "There's a few of them," that he's left.

---

[15] https://www.facebook.com/chriscornell/photos/a.116887764686.94354.5052659686/10153873077954687

[16] David's father; Haywood Jones. His mother Peggy said: "The midwife said, 'This child has been on this earth before'. I thought that was rather an odd thing to say but the midwife seemed quite adamant." David wore a cross given him by his father throughout his life. https://www.thesun.co.uk/archives/news/100710/i-think-i-have-done-just-about-everything-its-possible-to-legend-david-bowies-cosmic-life-remembered/

Letters that she'll find or has found?

"That she'll find."

I think he has some more music coming out.

My interpretation of what I'm seeing is love letters, but that could be a reference to music as well. I'm asking him, **"Are they love letters or music?"** He said, **"It's a combination."**

Anything you want to tell your fans, people who love and miss you?

"The music lives on. We've all heard that, but we should know that, as well."

How about you, Prince. Why did you show up to help Chris when he crossed over?

He was up there with the orchestra.

The music Chris was hearing? How is that created?

He saw him playing his song "Nothing Compares to U."

>(Note: Chris did record a version of that Prince song. We'll hear more about "frequencies of music" in subsequent chapters.)[17]

How is that image and sound created? How do you create music for Chris to hear?

It's instantaneous; it's a frequency that just goes "zoom" together at once. A frequency that goes back to his own

---

[17] https://www.youtube.com/watch?v=IuUDRU9-HRk

unique frequency and then he magnifies his (own) frequency.

Is that something you've always been able to do or something you learned over there?

He said "Yes, he's always known how to do it, but not consciously." He showed me being here, how he pulled the frequencies in here, but now, he realizes that he can do that up there. He now knows how to amplify and draw in others.

Anything you want to impart to us, Chris?

Chris wants us to talk about suicide... I asked him if he wanted me to bring that up in the radio show tonight and he said "Yes, absolutely." He says he was "playing Russian roulette" and not realizing it... doing things that were like playing Russian roulette; he didn't think he would die from it.

Suicide is such an important topic because as an act, it tends to inspire others in pain. We've got three suicides here – Prince from taking all that pain medication, Robin who was also suffering from a brain illness, but Chris, what was your hurry?

Chris is asking me something... Okay. He wants me to talk (more) about suicide. "It's not the way to go, it's very challenging for people over there to get through to people over here, and they're trying to figure out the best way to communicate... to talk them out of it."

You're suggesting Jennifer should talk about suicide; what should she say?

He just said, "Weren't you listening?" He said, **"Whether you're playing with drugs, even though you're not thinking that playing with drugs or things that can kill you,** (from cigarettes to whisky to heroin) **is about suicide, it is a form of suicide."**

> (Note: I love it when I get chewed out by people on the Flipside. "What, *weren't you listening?*" It's a funny idea and takes some of the sting out of what we're speaking about. "Wake up! Pay attention! I'm talking to you!")

How do we tell people to stop doing that?

He showed me my friend Dr. Drew.

Therapy?

He says, "What it (drugs) **does, is make your heart grow small, it makes your heart harden, your heart closes – there are drugs people use that make them feel more connected, but these kinds of drugs make it harder** (to do so)." **The first thing he said is "Your heart has the answers."**

Best drug in the world is to have your heart open?

"Best drug in the world is you. Life."

How can we get people to open their hearts and tap into the drug known as the heart? To tell people to stay away from drugs?

"They're not going to be able to hear it. Family members might hear it and help them, they're going through everything as well."

43

But Chris, would you have changed if your family had told you to stop toying with drugs?

He showed me the breakup was from something else... not about a relationship. He showed me... an imbalance. But now they're laughing and saying that they're all "chemically imbalanced." Except for David Bowie. He said, "He was not."

David, what did you learn from going through cancer, that journey through that illness to the flipside?

He learned how much he loved his wife and friends... He says "It made me learn to love life. The more you're connected to source, that's what opens up your heart."

Connect to source... how?

"Singing, acting, being creative. You make your heart fill with love and compassion, do things for other people and your heart slowly opens up."

Thank you. Okay, Robin, let's lighten up this mood. Can you tell us something funny? Maybe a flipside joke?

> (Note: Never asked anything like this before, had no idea if he'd say anything or Jennifer would respond.)

He says, "There are two blondes walking down the street. (Pauses. Listens) And they find an exit sign and they say, "No thanks, we don't want to leave."

Ha! Okay, a flipside blonde joke.

Why are my ears burning suddenly? He said "It's the frequency... he said "Please express that people who stay

here (on the planet and don't commit suicide) experience so much more than leaving.

(Jennifer listens) Chris says he **"No longer gets to give his daughter a kiss anymore."** He's saying, **"I don't get to breathe anymore."** Or that he doesn't get **"To worry about what's going to happen. That he doesn't get to play. It resonates. It's fun to be on the planet, to experience life. Don't be in a hurry to exit."**

Does Luana want to step in?

She says she's herding them. **She's says this class is going to change things.**

This class that she's officiating?

This is a class in communication between this side and that side.

Is there anything that you miss Luana? About being on the planet?

She pinched your cheek. She misses you, but then she doesn't because you're here. Um. **Did you guys have a convertible or something?**

Yes. I had a 1965 Mustang convertible when I met her.

She misses... "Driving in the wind, driving in a convertible and not giving a shit..." She showed me her cats... her cats are there with her.

(Ding! *A bell of verification.) Anyone else? Oh, what about Jan Sharp? The Australian film producer. Old friend. How's Jan?*

She's very elegant. She's holding a cigarette, a long one, like in a holder.

> (Note: Jan was one of the most elegant people I've met. During a between life session (in "It's a Wonderful Afterlife") I asked her about her journey, and she said she was "flying around galaxies exploring with her friends.")

Last time we spoke you said you were flying around having great adventures. How are you doing? I know her family might not be open this information.

She says, "Whatever they think is right."

You had so many pals, what do you do during the day?

"They're all over there." She says she writes. She shows me like making her own garden. She's showing me the sound of the birds, the way things smell, she's out in that garden writing. It's hard for them to manufacture all those things over there. We have nature and all of it, but they have to work at it.

> (Note: "Manufacture" is repeated often in these reports. The idea of experiencing something "over there" like drinking tea, relaxing on the beach, or singing, is a construct that has to be manufactured. When asked "How do you do that?" they often reply "Math.")

Can we access your writing?

"No." She told me "It's for her future self."

Anything I should tell members of your family?

Oh, good luck with that one. "Try to give more love."

You think they'll listen to me?

That's why she said, "Good luck with that one."

> (Note: Not long after this, her family did get in touch with Jennifer, and one of them had a session with her that was "amazing," as this family member put it. They were able to contact someone who passed years ago and gave them details no one else could have known. Afterwards, I heard that it was comforting to realize that those who are no longer on the planet are still accessible.)

Well, thanks Jan. I had a lot of fun knowing you, you were such a dramatic and wonderful person.

She was an actress too. She just showed me Nicole Kidman.

Really? (ding!) Nicole lived in her house.

Did you ever tell me that?

No, when Nicole first started in the business she lived at Jan and Phillip's home. When she made her first film "Dead Calm" with Jan's husband Phillip Noyce.

I had nightmares about that film. It was such a good film!

Any last words from anyone up there?

They love you.

Who said that?

Who do you think? Luana.

Okay class see you next week.

*****

This was the initial discussion of Luana moderating a class. Luana had shown up before, Prince and Robin Williams before, and we had various conversations with others.

But this was the first time the idea of her moderating a *"Translation class"* had come up. From this point forward, it became the structure of our conversations. If someone "showed up" we directed them to speak with or participate in some form of orientation – to see what it was that we were doing in the class.

All I can report is what Jennifer heard from her dad on the Flipside; **"It's not your job to prove that there is an afterlife. It's your responsibility to be as accurate as possible."**

Which is what we're doing. There are authors who "channel" celebrities, I've met a few people who claim to be "channeling" musicians. My thought is always to add the caveat, *"It feels to me* like I'm channeling this person's music. I have no idea if I am conversing with them or not."

The same goes for this book. It *feels* like Jennifer is communicating with these people, and when I hear contrary information I include it. I try to see if what they're saying is accurate – especially **"new information."** Like Chris Cornell saying he met Bowie briefly a long time ago, something I didn't know, but turned out to be accurate when I researched it. Little things Jennifer and I could not have known but is later proven to be accurate.

I know how odd this format is – *really*. I come from a world of formal story telling, writing for magazines and editors as well; "How can we fact check this?" Or movie studios poring over scripts to pass "Errors and Omissions." I toyed with the idea of making these conversations "anonymous" – "This is a person who was a famous rock star but had eyes different colors" - but they insisted I not do that.

Very odd to have someone on the Flipside say, *"It's important you report what you're hearing verbatim."* Some will reject it outright – but the people **who need to hear it,** will. If by reporting what they say offends any family member; I'm sorry for doing so.

Believe me – I know how many at this point will want to return this book. **I beg you, please do!** Give it back to whomever gave it to you or get a refund. We're not here to upset anyone's apple cart, or eBook "cart." **Ultimately its the answers that are important. Not who is saying them.**

If we can just focus on what is being said consistently – I've done this with a few mediums, while talking to people who are under hypnosis, or just asking questions while a person is fully conscious – it doesn't really matter what the method is **if we get the** *same answers.*

On one hand, I suggest trying to ignore **"who"** is speaking. See if *what they say* has any resonance with you. Try to "unfreeze your mind" about who *these people were* – and focus on what they're saying. And how it might relate to your own journey.

That is the value of listening to things that may seem crazy; the only way to verify the crazy things you're about to hear is how you feel when you hear them.

But if you stick around; *"Welcome to our class!"*

Luana Anders in another class; "Reform School Girl"

CHAPTER TWO:
HARRY DEAN STANTON

"Just open yourself up to the possibility that there might be an afterlife."

Harry Dean Stanton with his "Big Love" costar Bill Paxton. Photo: Variety.

This is a chapter about one session where my pal Luana Anders (who passed away in 1996) and her pal Harry Dean Stanton (who passed a few weeks prior to this meeting) explained his journey into the flipside. The conversation was filmed and transcribed and presented here.

First some bonafides; I've known the character actor Harry Dean Stanton ("*Paris, Texas*" "*Big Love*") since I appeared in an episode of "*Laverne and Shirley*" with him back in the 80's.[18] I played a pizza delivery guy who whenever he rang the doorbell, was always shy a couple of slices of pizza. "*Hey*

---

[18] Laverne & Shirley episode "Star Peepers" 1982

fur face, where's the rest of our pizza?" (Shirley's line) And I'd make up some story *"Well, I was on my way here, and suddenly I saw this fire in a building, and I set the pizza down, and went over to the building and caught this baby that fell out of window... but when I got back to your pizza, a few slices were missing."*

All the while, wiping pizza crumbs out of my beard.

Charles Grodin got me the part, it was his idea, he called his pal Penny Marshall and she brought me in to do an episode. I filmed the bit on the same night that Harry Dean Stanton was performing - singing songs actually, and later, when I ran into Penny she said, *"Oh, I forgot. We had to cut you. Harry's song went long."* (Some years later Penny and I shared the "millennium cruise" aboard Bob Shaye's yacht - and I played piano while Penny sang. So, there was a circle to that story as well.)

Harry and I jammed at a party one night - playing guitars, him crooning his Spanish repertoire - Harry knew them all. We also spent a night drinking at Dan Tana's with Dabney Coleman at their booth. We drank until the wee hours, smoking cigarettes outside; Harry was always friendly to me because of the Luana connection - but he firmly did not believe in an afterlife. He spoke of that disbelief often.

He was kind of famous for talking about it - this was the only path and journey, and after that, *nothing*. As the director of his most recent film Lucky points out: "He was deeply spiritual person who **was 100% certain that there was no God and there was only a void and we were all going to disappear into nothing and no one was in charge**," John Carroll Lynch says. *"He was deeply committed to that worldview."*

That is, until I spoke to him yesterday. On the Flipside.

Jennifer did not know who he was, did not know who I was referring to, and I carefully avoided saying his full name or credits or how he and Luana knew each other. But I suspected it might have been difficult for Harry to accept there IS an afterlife, since he was famous for being a skeptic about it... and finding himself "still alive after crossing over" would likely have given him *something to talk about*.

*****

Rich: Let's ask Luana how her friend, who just showed up this past week on the Flipside, is doing.

Jennifer: He showed up.

Let's call him Harry Dean, for the sake of this conversation. How is Harry doing? Do you know who I'm talking about?

No. I know nothing about Harry but let me find out – sounds like a sausage.

That's Jimmy Dean.

Luana just said "Oh, Richard."

Well, before we begin, let me tell you a little about Harry. He was like a philosopher, followed Krishnamurdi, basically believed there is no afterlife, that there is only this life.

That's why she said "Oh, Richard."

Did she greet Harry?

Yes. A week before he passed. She says he got things in order a week before he left. She helped him before he crossed over.

Anyone else helping him?

She showed me 5 people around him at his death.

> (Note: ***(ding!)*** I found out at his **memorial that five women were in the room with him when he crossed over. I didn't know this fact when Jennifer said it, but it later turned out to be accurate.**)

Male or female?

Female.

Who was there to greet him as he crossed over?

His mother was there to greet him – and a child. Did he have a child?[19]

I don't know.

This child is very young - either a baby that died right after it was born... or died before birth. I don't think he was married to the mother.

> (Note: **The five women who were with Harry when he died later claimed that he said to them "Hand me the baby" and they were aware he was seeing someone that they could not.** Again, another detail that was 100% correct, but said to me a week prior to learning it as his memorial.)

---

[19] Harry Dean Stanton was born in West Irvine, Kentucky, to Ersel (née Moberly), a cook, and Sheridan Harry Stanton, a tobacco farmer and barber. His parents divorced when Stanton was in high school; both later remarried. *Wikipedia*

So, is this child someone Harry Dean had with a girlfriend? And the baby didn't make it to term?

I'm getting that this happened in the 60's ... I'm getting 1962. I don't know if the mother was born in 1962 or the baby was born in 1962.

Was going into the afterlife a surprise for him?

He didn't accept it at first... because your belief system... whatever you believe is not wrong – "but if you believe that there's nothing... that's your belief." He tried to quantify it the best way he could.

"Tried to quantify it?" How?

That's what he said - he tried to quantify what he was seeing. He was there (on his deathbed) **with medicine, and the time he was leaving his body.**

Was he assuming the medicine was creating hallucinations?

Yes, he was trying to "document" it. Did he document things or was he known for that? It's like he was trying to find proof. Did he study it?

Yeah, he talked a lot about life and death, what happens and what doesn't. He investigated things deeply.

I felt like a lot of people were around his bed. I don't know if that was etherically or he was with family – but he was very loved.

Yes. That's sounds right.

"So loved," he said.

Luana tried to help him?

He tried to understand it – like he does with everything... again the word quantify comes to mind, he tried to assume that he was just like, you know, "stuck in his memory" kind of thing.

Who broke through to make him realize he wasn't?

She did.

How did you do that, Luana?

She held his hand. She told him he was safe. He says she "gave him a soft landing."

A soft landing. How does he appear now to you Lu?

She says he's "an old fart." That's her expression.

Funny, that was one of Luana's phrases.

He appears to be her age... around their 30's.

You and Harry Dean went on a trip together.

"Yes," they did. Santa Barbara? Somewhere up north. That's what she showed me... like on a road trip – she showed me she was wearing a hat and the car meant everything...

> (Note: Just prior to this conversation, I'd learned Luana, Harry Dean Stanton and film producer Fred Roos (very much alive) drove to the Monterey Pop festival in 1967 together. Their friends were making a film about it (later called "Monterey Pop.") I was at a screening of Monterey Pop, a film I'd never seen, and I texted Fred. "Didn't Luana go the Monterey Pop festival?" He wrote back "She and Harry Dean

Stanton and I drove up there together." When Jennifer is saying this, **I can't quite believe what I am hearing**, because I had just learned this fact some 50 years after the trip.)

Whose car was it? Was it Harry's car?

Felt like it was part ownership – like it was a studio's car or something.

> (Note: Fred Roos did not remember whose car they took, but said indeed, it "could have been someone from the film who provided it.")

Who else was in the car?

Was it like a brother? They grew up together... had the same background. Funny, I'm seeing an image of my husband Fred.

*Actually, **that is the third person's name**. I'm going to see this person Monday. Anything you want me to tell Fred when I see him?*

Luana blew hearts and kisses.

That's not enough for Fred.

"Tell Fred he's dehydrated. He needs to hydrate more."

> (Note: Jennifer said she "heard the sentence" but was reluctant to say it, as it sounds *so generic*. When I saw Fred the next Monday, he revealed that his son has been telling him that every day he needs to "hydrate more." He son pulled me aside and said "I read your email to Fred. I can't believe she said to tell him that. It's exactly what I've said to him daily.")

She's telling me he's very kind. And always roots for the underdog, but he's very stealth.

That's correct. Fred is taciturn and very private. They're old great friends. I'll tell you who they are afterwards.

> (Note: There's **no way** that Jennifer could know that is the description Fred would get from his closest friends. She's never heard of him, I didn't say his name, she did – and Fred Roos has given me permission to tell this story as it occurred.)

They loved each other. Fred is heartbroken at the loss of his friends.

He wrote me the other day and told me of this road trip the three of them went on.

They were late – something happened – a flat tire? There were several bumps in the road, that could be figuratively – what's the other guys name?

Harry Dean.

Like someone forgot something – they kept looking for it – felt like they were looking for something.

Ultimately, they did get where they were going. They went all the way up to Monterey.

Okay, I was seeing Santa Barbara... there was something going on. **A festival of some kind?**

What kind of festival?

She says, "It's a free spirit festival." She's showing me movie screens, something going on, they had to sit - then

showing me screens. That they had to take part of – it had to do with advertising of whatever it was.

> (Note: Fred and Harry Dean and Luana were invited by the filmmakers to take part in the film at the behest of Lou Adler and John Phillips (of the Mamas and Papas) who produced the film.)

She's saying they just did it for fun, it felt like a rave – showing me a bunch of bands playing. It was like one of the first of its kind, she's showing me. Like Lollapalooza? But no, this was way back when.

Do you remember any of the acts that you saw perform there?

I just got shown Prince. But I don't think he was there. I can't imagine how.

> (Note: When she said this I chuckled, knowing that Hendrix had performed at Monterey, how he was dressed at the show, and how Prince liked to wear some of the same outfits.)

*Look closer. Prince, or somebody **like Prince**? Is he playing an instrument?*

Yes. He's playing guitar.

Okay.

Oh. Was it Jimi Hendrix?

Correct.

She showed me Jimi Hendrix, but I forgot what his name was.

I got the reference. Prince dressed like Jimi sometimes. Let me ask Harry, you and I had dinner, well we had drinks with a friend Dabney (Coleman) one night. I was giving an old friend a tour of L.A., and ran into Harry at Dan Tana's; we drank...

"Until four in the morning," he said.

*Correct. **(ding!)** They wanted us to come with them to another bar - we bailed.*

> (Note: Another detail Jennifer would not, could not have known. As Harry was an honored guest, he and Dabney Coleman were allowed to stay much longer than after they closed at 2 a.m.)

We also played guitars together at Gina Gershon's party.

"For two minutes," he said.

That's about right. And.. you and I did a Laverne and Shirley together – I got cut out because your song went long.

He says he wishes he had got cut out as well.

Very funny. Listen ... you're an adorable fellow. What do you want me to... (before I can finish the question)

"There is an afterlife."

Is that what he wants me to tell... who, Fred?

Thank you, Luana. "Fred knows it."

And your friends?

"Go easy on his friends."

There's a mutual friend that we have if you look around this room that Harry Dean knows.

Bill Paxton, right? Bill showed up.

That's correct. Do you know consciously why they're together?

He's showing me (Harry is) like a mentor – it was a mentor relationship, like Bill was very young... had to do with something when they were younger.

> (Note: Bill and Harry Dean Stanton worked together on the HBO show "Big Love." Bill has shown up a number of times since his passing, including during an interview I was filming with another medium, which is the subject of a later chapter.)

What was it like for Bill to see Harry or Harry to see Bill?

Oh, they had a drink, they were like "What the fuck!? I can't believe this is happening."

Harry, what do you want you to me to tell your friends at your memorial? "There is an afterlife!" with an exclamation point?

"No, there's more than an afterlife."

So there is an afterlife, comma... "and there's more than an afterlife?"

"There is a present life that creates an afterlife."

What does that mean, Harry?

He showed me different levels, because he didn't believe in it, he spent a lot of time here mentally thinking about it

(while still alive.) He couldn't escape it; he's showing me like being on the bottom of the treadmill. "If you just believe there is an afterlife it will make you more present... versus fighting it."

You're saying if you just believe, it will make it easier for you?

"That if you believe, you can't be wrong."

Just believing?

"To just be open to believing. Just be open to it."

I'm going to craft a sentence like "Harry Dean says there is an afterlife, but he also said, "Be open to believing in an afterlife."

He showed me the song, **"Don't stop believing."**

Okay, that's funny. Well, he is a musician. So, Jennifer, you don't know who Harry is?

No. I don't have a clue, other than the sausage guy.

That's Jimmy Dean. But Bill knows who he is... and Luana has known him a long long time...

Did he have something to do with Star Wars?

> (Note: I think he's referring to Dan Tana's bar again – which he called "The Star Wars Bar" because of the mixture of characters who inhabit it. *"I don't like you, and my friend doesn't like you either."* Harry said in

an interview where he called it that. (Which I'd never heard until I searched for it online.)[20]

Right now I want to speak to Harry without thinking about who Harry is.

He knows a lot of people who are over there. He says, "It's been a reunion." Since the car ride, it's been a huge reunion – like that was one of his favorite moments in time. That was the event that actually convinced him he wasn't in a dream.

Was it Luana who brought him to that car ride? So he could experience it again?

He says he "got tricked into it." He got tricked into coming over. He thought (the car ride) was a happy memory and actually that was her way of helping him calm down. By showing him that car ride.

Wow.

By showing him the car ride, then he was open to what he was experiencing... But then he suddenly realized it wasn't just a happy memory.

At what point in the car ride did you realize it wasn't a memory?

When they had the flat tire. Because they didn't have a flat tire during the actual trip. When that happened he said, "What's going on?"

---

[20] Harry Dean calls Dan Tana's the "Star Wars Bar" https://www.hollywoodreporter.com/video/harry-dean-stanton-calls-dan-735518

Who did you say that to?

Fred.

Just to confirm this – Fred is still on the planet. But this other version of Fred, that you experienced in your dream, that's the portion of Fred's energy that he's left behind while he's incarnated here. Is that correct?

Harry said, "Fred's higher self." Then he said to me "Now do you see how confusing this is?"

Well I do. (Laughter)

He said, "The Fred up here is much less uptight than the Fred there." He said, "I knew that was a clue."

> (Note: *(ding!)* Sentence still makes me laugh. Fred is one of those people who listens with great intent, doesn't say much, is a giant in the film world. After casting "American Graffiti" and other epics, he went on to produce all of Francis Coppola's films, as well as his daughter Sofia's films. I've known him since Luana sent me in to meet him in the 80's at Zoetrope and found myself babbling for 30 minutes as he listened intently. At the end of my monolog he said, "You need to pay your dues." That Harry would describe Fred as "uptight over there, but not over here" is like ringing a giant cowbell of verisimilitude.)

Have you seen any of your other friends?

He shows me lots of friends; they all came to see him... He showed me the person who came to change a tire was like a Robin Williams – someone like that – that fucked him up

- then he realized it couldn't be a memory, that didn't happen – but the feelings were the same from that memory...

Amazing.

"That's a great way to trick someone into coming over."

To trick them to shifting their focus so it's not about fear... not about worrying or having fear of the afterlife.

He said, "He didn't believe in an afterlife, couldn't believe in the afterlife... he didn't want to believe. Said he was hurt by people leaving the planet, it was like he walled himself off from that emotion."

I understand.

He said "Luana was coming back and forth..."

Visiting him etherically?

"He thought it was a dream or a hallucination from the medicine he was getting."

How did she appear to you?

"She was wearing these striped pants with bell bottoms that went down and she had this big hat, same hat she had in the car ride."

So eventually you cross over and there she is – you're in the car and...

"And then there's a flat tire..."

Then you look at Fred and say, "But we didn't have a flat tire, and then he says, "I know!" It's at that moment you realize there is an afterlife. Okay, Harry let's show Jennifer who you are. You remember the patriarch in "Big Love?"

His dad?

Yeah, the old man in charge of all the girls.

That wore the bad suits that married a 12-year-old girl?

That's him. Harry Dean Stanton.

Wow. I loved that show. I had no idea.

Well, thanks for showing up Harry.

*****

So off I went to Harry Dean Stanton's memorial service. It was a small but packed audience who were treated to stories about Harry Dean's life and legacy. Attendees including his pals Jack Nicholson and Warren Beatty, Al Pacino, Rebecca De Mornay, Ed Begley Jr. and others.

When I entered the room, Fred Roos waved me over. His son confirmed details I had written to Fred in an email, and other key points – including some health issues with other attendees, which I dutifully passed along to them from their pal on the flipside.

For example, I had a specific message for one individual about getting his prostate checked. ("Hey, don't shoot the messenger!") I mentioned it to someone close to him, and she said, "He went in for his first treatment yesterday." There were other intimate details that were confirmed when I spoke to the people he wanted me to speak to.

As noted, there were five women at this event I had never met before, but I learned were at his bedside as he passed. They said Harry was "hallucinating" before he passed, and he specifically said "Hand me the baby" to one of them.

As if there was a baby in the room. The very same thing he told Jennifer a few days before.

I made a point of reporting to Harry during our next class with Jennifer.

*****

Jennifer: Luana is here.

Rich: What does she want to say?

Harry Dean is here. He's saying, "Thank you."

For what?

"For giving his friends the awareness, they're all chatting about it, making fun of it or not..." It's so funny; Luana is coaching him how to talk to me.

How is she doing that?

She showed me, like, taking him to the front of the class, the one who is next in line... escorting him to the front.

Ushering him forward?

Showing him the frequencies, how you project things... and she has to keep the class quiet, so we can hear her. (To Luana) "How do you do that?" (pause) I love her voice; this is the first time I heard her voice. It's very therapeutic.

How can we help people focus their energy, so they can communicate? Do we need to help the people over there focus their energy?

She's showing me the heart. And the frequency... so let's say... (pause) She's showing me like... since Harry doesn't know me Jennifer – but he knows what I know of him. He shows me what I know of him, things like (the HBO show) "*Big Love.*" That's how he "gets in" or a lock.

So that's the energetic image that he's using, so he can break down what the energetic pattern is? Like searching something on the internet, looking for patterns?

He shows me a cowboy hat... that he used to wear in the show. That's my version of "*Big Love*;" that old brown suit he wore. He's saying, "I'm sorry you had to see me like that, because I'm really a cool guy." He's showing me a guitar... I feel like he was singing.

That's correct. (ding!) A beautiful singer, he performed at The Mint on Pico often. He was known for his singing as well.

Oh, he is? He was showing me... it's different frequencies up there so that's why he was singing off key. He's funny.

His Spanish songs all drift tonally; they sound off key.

Like gypsy music...

Yes, Harry is famous for that... singer, yes, guitar player, "Big Love," yes.

He was trying to show me "You know me like this." Showing *me* for the lock.

68

Explain this, Luana and Harry, when he wants to communicate, what does he do? Create the image, or does Luana create the image?

They both do. She understands it more, so she can do that.

How do you see Jennifer, Luana?

She's showing me the back of my head.

Are you seeing Jennifer as a light?

"Yes. White. Everyone else is (appears) like different colors... all different colors."

But that little frame of Jennifer is unique... not just white, per se, but variations of white, so you can recognize it. People over there can access it with "Oh, that's Jennifer" correct?

"This light is in communication with that light. By me being open to talk to her or whomever she brings with her." I did ask Luana to "please be here today" to come today... and she's met my dad... She says, **"He is a better teacher now."** He was teacher, he loved to teach. And then Morton just arrived. What's his name?

Michael. (Michael Newton aka "Morton" is going to appear in a later chapter)

Newton. Funny, now everyone calls him Morton over there; they think it's funny. There are no names, really, people are nameless, but Michael is handling how more people elsewhere can learn from this process, based on what we do. Because our conversations are so open, we don't have fear associated with this. I asked Luana "How do you communicate? Is it just you (doing the talking)?" **She showed me everyone is doing it at once.**

Luana said **"We have a specific agenda of what we want you to learn or to know, by you being open, it's easy. But if we have more people projecting what we want you to do..."** for example they all have an image of Harry in "Big Love," and my dad is laughing because he was Mormon.

> (Note: For those who haven't seen *"Big Love"* it was an HBO series about an offshoot of Mormonism where they live outside the main community, but continue to practice plural wives.)

They knew I haven't seen Harry before - Luana was doing the communicating. But the communication is coming from everybody – everyone that knows Harry is with him.

Rich: Has "access" to him?

Jennifer: They all have access to him and are able to mastermind what they want to convey to us. Like when (we were talking to Harry before) **I saw Prince; he was showing me his memory of seeing Jimi Hendrix but that translated to my seeing Prince in my mind.**

In terms of accessing the image in our brain, what's the operational system? How do they access our memory, so they can transmit an image?

She showed me the picture I just saw. The way that they access it (is) **they put it in your head or my head; what pops up in our mind is from our knowledge, that's the vision they see. "Harry Dean in his dark suit"** – and that's what they use.

Let me ask; a photo captures time and space...

Captures a frequency.

Right, but when we access that frequency...

It has so much reality in it. The reality is in it. It's so much more work over there than here.

Well, that's the question. It's like a hologram. A hologram retains all the elements of the photograph, so if you break apart a hologram each piece will have all the same information the original had. Having a photo in front of us is captured time and space, and by looking at it, that's the thing you would use to search for somebody, because you're looking at that photograph and scanning the universe for the frequency or energetic pattern. So isn't the photo also a portal? Can you use a photograph to access that person in real time?

It's like a calling card. When I'm accessing this information, with Harry for instance, it sends out a frequency to everyone who knows Harry over there, everyone who ever knew him... and it makes a strong link to help us here. It's like me calling them all up; only they are the ones that gave me the idea to call them up.

Like they sent out the image of that person or name and then you call upon them.

You're correct about the portal, like when a picture appears, when you see that picture, it's accessing that particular time and space and those feelings or frequencies that are associated with those people in the photograph.

When I do the kind of focused memory work that I do with people, I often ask them to remember a photo. Once they do, I try to shift the tense to present tense, to address the memory as if it still exists, like a hologram. By doing so, I can ask them to look around themselves, and see what it's like to walk up to, or into the hologram.

Bingo. "You've got it wired here," they said.

Let's see if we can figure out how we can create some mode or mechanism, so people can access their loved ones using this method.

I just heard applause. I wish while you're filming me, you could see what I'm seeing while you're talking. They know I'm not going to remember this, talking to them is like a dream state for me... it's me in a dream state that later I can't remember.

That's why I'm filming this. Ok. In terms of "How can we create some method, perhaps an application, or an institute that helps people access their loved ones..."

Quantifying it.

But does a photo or a hologram give us the portal?

Or (use) **a memory – memories create all that.**

I wonder if there would be a tangible way to do that – You know, "upload your photo to this website, and we'll help you to access those people and ask them direct questions."

Morton says he wishes he would have done that down here. All the sessions would have been cut in half, like what you're doing in your coffee shop conversations...

(Note: I refer to them as coffee shop conversations, because we're fully conscious while visiting the Flipside in these conversations, often while drinking coffee.)

The second question...

They said, "You've already asked four."

It's only one! Is it correct, when accessing the energy of a person, we access that energy in relation to how we knew the person. For example, I may know someone as a boy in this life, but others may have known them as a girl in some other lifetime, but you'd present yourself as a boy to me, and a girl to those others who know you that way. Is that correct?

"Yes." I'm not following you, but he says "Yes."

How can we harness that energy so we can help people access you guys over there?

Focus on the heart.

It's my understanding that when we come here, we have filters or limiters on our consciousness, so we aren't aware of other information, past lives, other realms, etc. Where do those filters exist? In the brain, outside of us, in the geometric shapes so many have spoken of... or are they some form of a chemical imbalance in the brain?

It's whatever your belief system is; that controls those filters. Whatever your belief system is, affects those filters.

Is there a physical barrier that exists?

They're showing me an energy field.

Okay. So who put that barrier up?

If we didn't have those barriers, it would scare the shit out of people who don't have them.

You mean like, I would look around at people and remember them from previous lifetimes. Like, "I recognize this waiter, he killed me the 15th century." Because it's too much information to process?

Hold on. Let them talk. (Jennifer laughs) I can't focus when you're talking.

Sorry.

It's both; we put up the filter, they put up the filter. Hmm. I wonder what that makes me? I don't have any filters; I'm very porous to everything that comes through.

Were you born that way, did you achieve that or was that given to you?

They showed me a member of the council handing out a medal that represents that quality or that portal. Like the star that Tony (Stockwell) **had.**

> (Note: In these sessions where people visit their "council" the counselors often are wearing some token that represents a quality of "advancement" that the person has earned. They represent that quality while appearing on their council. It might be a symbol of "courage" or "patience" or some other virtue. She referring to a session where the medium Tony Stockwell said he saw a "star" on his council member, and the star represented the ability to "travel through realms.")

74

So you Jennifer have one of those stars?

It represents (qualities I've learned over) **500 thousand years... over time. Which doesn't exist.**

Well there is time over "there," it's just relatively different.

They showed me a pulse.

Like an energetic wave?

They just showed me (time is) **like an X-Ray machine,** (with) **the energetic patterns. They said before I came, before I entered this place, my main objective was to not... was to be able to do this** (mediumship) **work without being killed.**

> (Note: In Jennifer's past life regression and between life session with Scott De Tamble, she remembered several lifetimes where she was either persecuted for witchcraft or was the persecutor of someone accused of it.)

Is there a method for people to undo the filter in our minds that don't allow access to this information? I would guess the answer is no – because tampering with the filter would alter a person's path or journey. But then sometimes people have a near death event, or take LSD and that alters the filter, correct?

It helps.

Is there a methodology to altering those filters through meditation, LSD, hypnosis?

Or plant medicine (ayahuasca).

Where you can stop the filters for a short amount of time, so you can access this information and then go back to living your life?

Some people are just not meant for it. I asked Luana "Is there a methodology?" and she said "No."

I'm getting it's like a VIP club... there is no hierarchy involved, but if you're not supposed to be accessing this information, or you discover something bad happened to you in a previous lifetime that effects you in this lifetime... it's not for everyone.

Let me ask Luana, do you direct people to us? If so, how do you do it?

She said, "Yes." She did this (wiped her forehead) **"It's exhausting."**

What's the process?

She's showing me a computer, looking at something, whispering into their ear, whoever it is, they make them focus. Like if you see a sign, you see a butterfly or a number, they put your awareness toward that. It's not that they are the butterfly reincarnated but are putting your awareness towards it. It's the same thing with a computer; people will figure it out, you're looking something up, (on the flipside) **they're going to help you with search keys...**

So you're the google in the googling?

Yes. They are *the google*. They said, "It's the ethernet." The etheric net.

So the internet mirrors something that already exists between all souls and people?

The ethernet influences the internet.

People through history have been afraid of sharing dreams or this kind of research; they'd be burned at the stake or dunked. So how can we help someone who is ill or needs our help mentally?

They're showing me Buddhist monks.

We need to consult monks to help with prayer?

No. They have a prayer chain up there with monks chanting up there to help people down here. Just like we do here.

Let's talk about that. Luana was a Buddhist, she was SGI, got Tina Turner involved in Buddhism.

I'm seeing white. With the white robe?

That's correct.

> (Note: Soka Gakkai is a Japanese Buddhist religious movement based on the teachings of the 13th-century Japanese Buddhist lama Nichiren. It is the largest of the Japanese new religions and holds the largest membership among Nichiren Buddhist groups. "The Gakkai" bases its teachings on Nichiren's interpretation of the Lotus Sutra and places chanting "Nam Myōhō Renge Kyō" at the center of devotional practice. Nichiren Shōshū priests distinguish themselves from those of most other schools by wearing only white and grey vestment robes and a

white surplice, as they believe Nichiren did."
Wikipedia)

She showed me that. I have no idea what that is.

When Luana was dying, I reached out to her friends at SGI and a prayer group came over and chanted for her until she passed. I know she appreciated that.

She loved it. Her frequency was amazing because of it.

But that energy of chanting?

"It's more powerful than any other."

I often compare the chant "Nam Myoho Renge Kyo" to the Tibetan "Om mani padme hum." Both mean basically "Praise to the knowledge of the Lotus Sutra," a teaching Buddha gave which discussed that all phenomena that we encounter is inherently not real.

I'm hearing that there's a higher frequency with one of them.

Do you mean by "higher"- a better frequency?

No. She said, "There's no hierarchy." She said, "The frequency is different." She actually clarified that while you were speaking; I asked, "Is it better?" **She said, "No it's a different frequency." She says because whatever it is that was associated with it, the energy has dropped with its use. It used to have more immediacy but has diminished over the centuries... something that is not current.**

Nam Myoho Renge Kyo is around 400 years old, while the Tibetan saying is much older, perhaps a thousand years old. One is used as a tool for people to obtain some form of enlightenment, used in prayer ceremonies, while I've heard in Tibet by people observing every day events or even as a way of saying "Praise be." Anything I can pass along to those who are chanting, something that will enhance their experience?

"They have to give it meaning other than just chanting. Some people just chant because its habitual."

Okay let's ask about that – let's call it a prayer.

Luana is saying "They didn't have this in a classroom. I'm not prepared!"

Let's say you're a Buddhist praying or chanting, a Catholic praying, or a Mormon praying...

"You have to direct that intention."

How do you do that?

"By creating the image that you're thinking of, or the outcome of the action of the person that you've got in focus."

Both?

"The action works better for the finished part. The finished part is them being healed."

So a projection in your mind, including a prayer of them being healed, seeing them in that healthy state?

"Let the universe deal with it; hand it over to them. It's like handing the keys to cops to drive your car, when you've had too much to drink."

But people are afraid of giving up the keys as earthlings.

"We have to... create paths for them to follow with our intent. She's showing me these roads – how when people pray, or chant, they create the energetic pattern, so they (on the flipside) **need those paths that we create in order to help us. It's the only way for them to hone in on our prayer, it's the only way for them to gain access to help us.**"

Let's say people pray for someone to live and they don't - how can we help people understand this process?

"**The soul knows... the soul knows this person and time... sometimes it does work, it does help, and that healing brings everyone in that awareness. But the time of death is always chosen by our souls.**"

You allow people to have their journey and path, but prayer helps them?

"**Chanting, praying, healing; fixing. It heals them,**" she says. She's very direct. "**It heals them with their participation. In the end it heals the person who prays or chants, the action helps the person they're chanting for.**"

"**All the masters have taught us, "set your intentions," but they're saying, "Just feel it now." Feel what you want as an outcome, because that gives them a quicker road map to help you get there.**" I'm going to ask Luana a different question, "Why are people so stuck?"

Stuck with what?

Feeling stuck, I find it a lot. (pause) **She showed me smoke; called it "ethernet pollution."**

What does that mean?

I'm asking her... "It's a metaphor." A kind of pollution of the mind that keeps people from accessing the ethernet (flipside) themselves. "**If you don't accept who you are or the shape you're in, your body, everything else, you feel trapped down here. If you're looking for a better body or something else better, it's a smoke screen in your mind.**"

What do you mean by the ethernet?

"**The ethers.**"

Clearing up the smoke so the flipside is clear?

"**Yes.**"

It gets smoke filled when your mind gets smoke filled?

"**Your mind here gets "smoke filled." You are exactly where you are supposed to be where you are currently, so don't put up smoke screens or worry about what you *should have been*. Just allow yourself to feel the way that you're going to be in the future.**"

Is the smoke screen related to self awareness or praying for something, trying to help yourself; I need a car, a job, is that where the smoke comes in?

"**All the fears come in. The smoke is fear.**"

I'm trying to keep this as practical as we can make it. So let's tell people "Here's a one, two three..."If you love yourself or others unconditionally there's no smoke?

"**Yes.**"

How do we help people effect positive change in their lives through intention or prayer?

Luana showed me the road map. She showed me being in that place of serenity, by staying in that place of grace, of love and light. If you're in that space and feel that intention, the end point of where you want to be, they're going to help you get to that place...

"It's a form of inception. They're putting that thought in your mind, they're projecting where you're supposed to go, if you're open to it. Then, if you have no filters, are able to be in the present, to be in the now – and are not having anything else effect it or interfere; that gives it the clearest road map."

Very cool.

"People have to be open in order to receive it. When your heart is open in this dimension you get everything, when your heart is closed you get shut off. It shuts off the frequency that allows you to conceive of things."

Well, I'd argue that we can't walk around being open all the time; we need to get out there and mix it up. Otherwise we won't learn anything, this place would be boring.

"It takes hundreds of thousands of years to be in this time. To arrive to this moment."

I saw this article about a statue made by an artist 40,000 years ago that was found in France. That human – were they any different than the humans on the planet now? This human who created this little piece of art back then is no different than anyone on the planet. Is that correct?

"No."

How so?

Hold on. **"That person is free from judgment."**

We tend to think of people 40,000 years ago as being less intelligent than now. I guess my question is if this artist is no different than artists now.

They just showed me an army of Richards.

That's funny. What's that? A sign of the apocalypse?

I asked Luana, "So why is Richard here?" She said, "He's a translator for all dimensions. You have no fear of expressing it at all despite what's being thrown your way. You have no fear."

You mean "I have no career" so I have no fear of losing it. It's not like I can lose one by following this research.

But you win awards *up there*. Because of what you've done here and standing your ground... you've won everything up there. (Jennifer to me:) I know it doesn't matter to you.

*It sounds funny. "I'd like to thank the members of the Academy and everyone who **was** a member of the Academy."*

"You wouldn't have been effective if you had been successful. That wasn't your plan."

> (Note: The artist's dilemma: if you're successful, you become bored or focus on the things that bring stuff; ego, vanity.)

Okay, see you on the flipside Lu.

She just did a chest bump.

A chest bump!   *****

CHAPTER THREE:
HARRY DEAN REDUX

"The Concierge of Connectedness"

Harry Dean Stanton and Friend

After the two previous sessions, I spoke to a friend about what I had learned from Harry Dean. He was so convinced that I was on the right track, that he asked me to ask Harry Dean a personal question. The next time we met, I did so. As usual, we sat in a noisy restaurant, me with camera in hand, Jennifer listening as I say, *"So who's in class today?"*

*****

Jennifer: Luana just came back. She helps organize my thoughts...

Rich: Here's my question to Luana... this memorial service for Harry Dean was hilarious; we all had fun.

She said "You should have seen the parade upstairs, dancing, lots of smokers...

A mutual friend had a question about Harry Dean's house.

Selling it or not. He's telling me, "There's a trust..."

*Correct. **(Ding!)** He wanted to know if his son should purchase the house.*

(Shakes her head, no.) Let's look at it from another angle...

"No," is fine. I can tell him that.

He's telling me "There are too many things involved, it's complicated. Too many attachments." Luana just threw in the word "Probate."

There's too many...

"Pots on the stove."

Should he try to navigate that?

This in interesting, usually they tell me "Yes," or "Go ahead and navigate." But instead Luana is very...

Precise?

"It's going to expose something by trying to navigate it... That's what needs to happen to get the ball rolling; otherwise it'll be tied up for a long time."

So the answer is "It's difficult, might be impossible, tied up in probate, but worth the effort to untie it?"

"Him getting involved is going to help them."

But he might not be able to get the house?

Right. But it will open it up... Harry just showed up. He's saying that... of course Bill Paxton shows up just after that; Luana keeps them all back. What does "easy writer" mean?

Luana, can you show Jennifer what that phrase refers to?

She's showing me a stage, like a set of some sort, a movie set... my mind goes to a movie set.

What's on the movie set? People?

I'm getting she's holding papers, notes, dialog... in a movie... it adds up to a movie.

Allow that to be the reality.

"Easy Writer" was a movie?

Correct. Except it was spelled Rider. "Easy Rider." Luana was in it, along with many of her pals.

Oh, I'm sorry! **I've never seen it.**

> (Note: Suffice to say, when I saw it in 1969 at the age of 14, I was blown away by it. I saw it maybe a dozen times. And then oddly enough, I met pretty much everyone in it or who worked on it. From Jack to Bert Schneider the producer, to Peter Fonda whose daughter starred in my first film, to Henry Jaglom an assistant editor, to Dennis... Karen Black and on and on. I don't know why I got to know them all – certainly I met most of them through Luana, but when I think back on the film, I can't help but marvel at how many of them I've come to know in my lifetime.)

Luana and I were in Boston once, at a bar on Beacon Hill. A group of backpacking kids joined our booth, and as they sat down we went around the table introducing ourselves and when Luana said her first name, a French girl said; "Luana? As in Luana Anders?" Luana smiled; "That's me." The girl nearly fainted. She had worked at the movie theater in Paris which showed "Easy Rider" non-stop for 30 years. And now here she was meeting Luana in person.

Luana said **"It was fun to make."**

We went to an Easy Rider reunion together in Santa Fe.

She said, "You broke her heart."

> (Note: I was taken aback by this sentence. No one wants to hear from their loved one on the Flipside how they had "broken their heart." But prior to this event in Santa Fe, Luana and I had split up – as boyfriend and girlfriend. It broke my heart as well. But it was something we had discussed, even "planned" for in our relationship. But somehow, we came back together six months later, when this reunion happened, and she invited me to accompany here on the trip. Jennifer had no way of knowing this detail. Still is gives me a jolt just typing this sentence.)

This is where I repaired it.

I don't know why she said that.

I do. We had broken up after ten years together. And for six months we were apart, even though I tried to stay in touch with her. Finally, she invited me to this "Easy Rider" reunion, and we flew out together and picked up our friendship where it left off. Peter Fonda, Dennis Hopper were there, we hobnobbed and laughed, first time she laughed since we broke up – so funny she mentioned that...

> (Note: That Thanksgiving, the first one we spent apart in ten years, she sent me a photo of her sitting alone at the table at the Coppola home looking like the loneliest person on the planet. Years later, Francis Coppola suggested to her that perhaps our breakup was responsible for her cancer, she said she told him, "Oh no, Richard is my best friend on the planet."
>
> We spent ten years together, six months apart, then ten more years as best friends. Truth be told, I now know why we felt that way about each other because I've seen during a between life hypnosis session that we had a lifetime together in the distant past. I explained it in "Flipside." It's hard to understand the depth of emotion I associate with her; I haven't seen her in 30 years and ***even typing this sentence pulls me into that well of emotion***.)

Since she brought it up... I'm having a side bar with her – I can't wait to meet her after listening about her in your audible book "Flipside" for 7 hours.

So what was my role in breaking your heart?

She fans herself.

Was there some logic for it?

"Your wife and the two kids..." She set you up.

Luana called me one day in a panic, her kitty Mr. Bailey had escaped. Luana was confined to her bed at the time, so my then girlfriend, later wife Sherry and I raced to her house. I went into the back alley and shouted for a half hour, when I came back, the cat was in Sherry's arms. Sherry had gone into the backyard and said "Mr. Bailey. Luana really needs you." The cat appeared in a tree above her and jumped into her arms. When I returned, Luana looked at me, locked eyes with mine, and said: "Sherry is an angel." Not an opinion, as if she was revealing something to me.

Luana knows what she did. She's giving you validation of her being here by telling this story... that's the only reason she's telling this... "They (she and Harry Dean Stanton) **can't wait for Jack** (Nicholson) **to get there."**

Let's not be in a hurry to send Jack anywhere. Okay, anyone else in class want to weigh in?

Paxton. He's being a gentleman with me. He says he wants to say "Thank you" *to you,* **for sending** (a link to) **his family... Even though you didn't get feedback, he says two people got it.**

> (Note: Bill Paxton gets his own chapter coming up. He was a friend of mine, and close to Harry Dean and others we're going to interview. I wrote a blog post about talking to him on the anniversary of his passing, but we will get to Bill in a few.)

Okay. Not sure if his family believes me or not.

It's not your job to make anyone believe... I question it all the time, as do you. But our job is to just report what we hear.

Agreed.

My dad is here... I feel like he's helping me with my work. He says he's learning from you.

Thanks Jim. I think we should get back to our crew... Anyone want to bring something up?

Prince is so sad about this Vegas shooting. It's dividing everyone.

> (Note: Jennifer had a client who was in Vegas during in the shooting and survived. She said she felt a strong presence of her deceased father during the event, and later in this book, Jennifer talks about it.)

Isn't that part of our journey on this stage of life? We can't learn without conflict, right?

Yes. We can. They're doing a general consensus...

But conflict is the essence of drama... otherwise there will be just "love all the time."

They're all laughing with that. (pause) **They're saying it doesn't have to be that way...**

There doesn't have to be conflict?

"Natural disasters, that's conflict;" they're saying that creates a lot of different lessons, we don't need to learn by people shooting each other...

If we asked him, the shooter... if we asked the people who died – would we find that they discussed this prior to coming here?

That's true.

So they wanted to teach lessons in love?

"Yes..." They say, **"Yes," but I'm just shown... like the Holocaust... I feel like we didn't have to go through that, even though...**

Even though we signed up for it?

Yeah.

> (Note: In "Flipside" the initial "between life session" I filmed was a woman who remembered dying in Auschwitz. (I was able to track the name her details.) But during her hypnosis session, she asked "Why did I choose such a difficult life? I lost everyone I loved." She said (it's also in the film "Flipside") "My guides are showing me that from a soul's perspective, it was harder to choose to play the role of a perpetrator than a victim." She went on to say that "every day in the camps was a heightened lesson in love, forgiveness, courage or compassion. From that perspective, seeing how difficult those roles were, I'm glad I chose the role that I did." It's a common refrain in these reports; "everyone chooses their lifetime to learn or teach lessons." It's not my theory, belief or opinion they say these things; it's just what they report consistently.)

Anyone else? Harry Dean... any observations about your memorial party?

"Too short."

I talked to your ex, Rebecca De Mornay... You were with her for a long time?

He says, "He met her when she was a little girl..."

(Note: It was on the set of *"One From the Heart"* which Luana worked on with her pal Francis Coppola writing "extra dialog." (He directed her in his first film "Dementia 13.") Rebecca was the "understudy" for Teri Garr but fell in love with Harry Dean while shooting that film. Rebecca told me there were together for 12 years. Jennifer wouldn't know this detail. Rebecca is in the credits of the film as an "understudy.")

It's funny about "Easy Rider" – it's the thing that brought me and Luana back together. I was 14 when I saw it, and then basically met everyone in the movie – the producer, director, most of the actors. I'm not connected to the film in any way except for Luana, and yet it's been a big part of my life.

"It was a springboard."

Luana is in the film, appears in a scene with Peter Fonda; it ends with violence.

Don't tell me! I haven't seen it.

Dennis Hopper directed it.

He's here.

Hi Dennis. Anything you want to say? You understand what we're doing?

"No." (Jennifer listens, looks at my camera.) **He says, "He's filming it from the other side."**

We're interviewing people no longer on the planet. When you crossed over, Dennis, who was the first person to greet you?

"His mom. Then his dad, but they didn't have a (close) relationship..." [21]

So Dennis, you and I chatted...

"In Venice."

That's right. **(Ding!)** *Both our kids were going to the same preschool and we talked about a mutual friend. Who was your first girlfriend?*

"In high school."

> (Note: Realizing that while I knew that Dennis was Luana's first boyfriend, that didn't mean she was *his* first.)

Is there anyone in this room that you've had sex with?

"Luana."

(Ding!) You were her first; she wrote about that in her script "Acting Up."

He says, "She wrote a very funny scene."

About something that didn't quite work?

"Yeah." (Jennifer laughs)

---

[21] January 12, 2007 "Marjorie D. Hopper, 89, passed away from complications from an infection... she married her high school sweetheart, Jay Millard Hopper. They had two beloved children, Dennis Lee Hopper and David Jay Hopper." CountryHistorian.com http://www.dodgeboard.com/forums/index.php?threads/dennis-hoppers-mothers-obit.2915/

> (Note: The script depicts her acting class that included Jack Nicholson, Robert Towne, Sally Kellerman and Dennis as his career was beginning. There's a running conversation with her pal Sally about losing her virginity, and Luana wrote the funniest scene I've ever read where she loses hers to Dennis. But Jennifer would not, *could not* know that. An example of a "bell ringing verification.")

Anything you want me to pass along? Your son is an actor...

"Be kind. Be love."

What have you learned on the other side?

"Traveling. Fast, man. And you can't travel in the same vibration you want to go. That's your security card."

Who do you hang out with on the flipside?

"My dog."

What's his name?

"Babe. He's a small dog... it's because he was short, we got a small dog to make him look bigger."

Luana wrote that in her script (about Dennis. He used to be sensitive about his height).

I didn't know that.

> (Note: I found in an article with Dennis talking about his beloved dogs – his first was a gift from the nearby Clutter family (that was the subject of the murder epic *"In Cold Blood."*) He says his "first dog was a

sheepdog," a gift from them. No idea what his dog's name was.)[22]

I spoke to Robert Towne the other day – any message for your pals back here? How about you, Dennis?

"Unfortunately," he says, "None of them believe in it (the afterlife). **Luana does, but she's over here. But it's a time thing."**

Luana, I quoted you as calling him your golden boy in one of the books. When Dennis crossed over, I heard your voice in my head saying, "He's my golden boy" and I saw this image of him shimmering with light... was that accurate?

(She laughs.) I'm being shown (a movie star) and something to do with a golden shower... (Snickers) They're laughing. **Dennis says, "He was ready for it, he was ready to leave."**

He sent a lovely bouquet of flowers to Luana's funeral.

He says, "The biggest. Duh."

Well actually Jack Nicholson's was equally as big... So, tell me about how you "arrived" on the flipside. How did you land?

He just showed me that he landed like he was tumbling over and over (gestures) **like this. But he felt ready for it.**

Who do you connect with (still) over here?

---

[22] https://www.huffingtonpost.com/alex-simon/great-conversations-dennis-hopper_b_7456112.html

His daughter. And she has kids. One is like a little Dennis... could be like a Dennis junior.[23]

There is a son... a daughter that went to school with our kids, probably around 14... he's keeping an eye on her?

"Always."

Luana, what are you doing over there?

She's connecting people. She's saying she's like "a concierge of connectedness."

Anyone else?

Robin Williams. There's an anniversary associated with Robin – soon. **He says "Tell people to focus on the light. And not the darkness, because the light is what's going to bring everybody up... to navigate our future... (pause) by focusing on the dark, and the bad things that are happening, you just stay there." He says "You don't have to forget (problems) but focus on all the things you can do something about. Focus on the things that are light... that's what's going to bring it all up, because that's what truly conquers the room. Focus on the light. I think people can understand that."**

What's the source of that light?

The heart. He just showed me the light. **"That's the frequency," he says.**

---

[23] https://en.wikipedia.org/wiki/Dennis_Hopper He reportedly has two grandchildren.

Is that the mechanism that allows us to communicate with the light? The heart is like a star trek communicator?

He just did his Mork and Mindy hand sign. He says, "Love is light... if you don't have a heavy heart, you're able to fly, you're able to connect more (to here)."

As he said to us in "Hacking the Afterlife;" "Love love."

(Jennifer pauses) He's just waiting for you to finish. He says, "We're the wave of the ocean within the source. The ocean is source, we're all a part of it, each wave is someone different, we all come back to it."

You mean the ocean as God or source?

Let me ask him. "How would you describe God?" (Jennifer pauses) He said "It's like water. If you don't have it, you die, if you live in an area where water isn't clean, people die, our bodies are made up of water."

My son pointed this out; "water doesn't die, it reincarnates."

"We are the wave and we all come back to it."

Any last words for our class?

They say "Always act through love; don't waste any time not doing that with yourself or others. Regardless of what you feel like, look like, or anything."

And others?

And others. "Time is of the essence in this dimension."

Do you mean our dimension or their dimension?

"Our dimension - which effects their dimension." (Jennifer aside) Interesting it's not the other way around.

The more love we express here, helps you folks out on the flipside?

"Yeah."

Is that some motivation to kick our ass a little bit?

They do (try), but nobody is listening.

I'd argue that we come here (to the planet) to learn lessons in love but we can't learn unless we come here to learn.

"You were born with it, but you forget it."

So we come here and suffer, conflict, suffer, conflict, little laughter, some high fives, then boom we're dead?

(Laughs.) They're saying **"That's so dismal. You just made it worse. You made it feel like a retirement community."**

Well, they are, a bunch of old peeps.

"They're not old now; they're young." They're showing me themselves as young. They're saying **"By loving more, you open up that space that allows more. It's a very basic mathematical equation that they're making. To get more love open yourself up by giving more love."** That's funny. I see Luana's wearing bell bottoms and a thing around her head, a laurel wreath.

Hippie heaven. Okay, we've got to run, there's the class bell. Anyone we missed we'll catch you on the flipside!

*****

CHAPTER FOUR:
INTERVIEW WITH MORTON

"He's over your shoulder."

Michael Newton in a still from the film "Flipside"

When I began this research into the Flipside a decade ago, I had planned a documentary about the topic, and was going to include Michael Newton as one of the subjects. But once I dove into his work, I realized what he was saying was *all encompassing*. I reached out to the Newton Institute to see if he was available for an interview on camera. I was told that he'd retired but I was welcome to film their conference in Chicago.

At the conference, Michael agreed to grant me his "last interview." It was nearly ten years before he ultimately passed away, but he actually said; "This will be *my last interview.*" I thought he was referring to a long line of filmed interviews that never seemed to go anywhere – but in retrospect he may have been referring to *the last filmed interview he was going to do on the topic.*

He was engaging, funny, and we spoke for over an hour. I got the chance to interview his wife Peggy as well, and she gave me perspective into her husband's research. I asked, *"So what did you think when your husband came home with these tales of a life between lives?"*[24]

She said *"I thought he was crazy. I thought they were going to take him away in a padded wagon... Until he shared the tapes with me. I realized all these people coming from all these walks of life were saying the same things about the afterlife."*

I realized that I needed to see or create my own "tapes" by filming people under hypnosis. The hypnosis sessions last anywhere from 4 to 6 hours and as reported in my books, they're a "wild ride into the flipside."

But I only met Michael the one time. I became friends with a number of people he trained, they all had stories about him, all admired him greatly. I was happy when he emailed me how much he liked my film "Flipside" which was about him and his work. He wrote: *"We viewed "Flipside" last night (he and Peggy) and we were blown away about how good it is. The visual lead-ins were just outstanding; I loved the way you interspersed visual images and graphic illustrations of the topic being discussed. The care taken in putting it all together really shows."*

He's a stickler for detail; I was worried he might not find it up to his standards. I was glad he loved it. But in order to understand the architecture of the flipside – and what I'm

---

[24] Peggy Jene Newton is Registered Nurse in California, and practiced 42 years from 1970 up until 2012

basing my questions on, he gives an excellent overview of his research in this excerpt from his interview in "Flipside."

INTERVIEW WITH MICHAEL NEWTON

Rich: Is hypnosis a valid scientific tool?[25]

Michael Newton: A lot of people don't feel it is. Hypnosis is a study of human behavior; adequate scientific proof depends on your willingness to accept self-reports from the mind as data. When someone is in deep hypnosis, it's not something that can be programmed. Under hypnosis, people are very aware of who they are and have great insight into what they're telling you. **Over thousands of cases there was consistency of reporting; it didn't matter whether a client had a deep religious belief system or not; once we had them in deep hypnosis, they all told us the same things.**

What was your first past life regression?

I began practicing in 1956, a traditional therapist using hypnosis to try to uncover childhood emotional and physical trauma. It was the year of the famous Bridey Murphy case - the Colorado housewife who remembered a previous life in Ireland. I'd get calls, "May I come for a past life regression?" I'd say "No, I'm traditional, not involved with "new age" thinking." I was very naive, really.

But then a client asked if I could see him about pain he was feeling in his side. He'd been troubled since childhood, and doctors said it was psychosomatic - they'd done x-rays and could find no physical symptoms. They told him he should

---

[25] excerpted from "Flipside: A Tourist's Guide on How to Navigate the Afterlife" "Interview with Michael Newton."

see a psychiatrist. When he came, I couldn't find any earthly origins at all, so I gave him the command "Go to the origin of this pain."

Well, he jumped into the life of a soldier in World War I, when he was a British Sergeant and was being bayoneted. I couldn't believe it; this fellow was lying on the couch groaning while I was more interested in verifying if it was real – asking him the British unit he claimed to be with and a number of other facts - instead of desensitizing this horrible trauma he was going through. Eventually I did do that.

He called a few days later to say, "There's no more pain, thank you." Well that didn't satisfy me, so **I contacted the British war office and the Imperial Museum in London to find out if this British Sergeant ever existed and sure enough he died in 1916. From that case, I began taking past life clients.** So I came kicking and screaming into this movement.

Sometime later, a woman came to me, depressed over having no friends and couldn't seem to connect with anybody. I reached a point of frustration when I couldn't seem to find any help, so I said, "Go to the origin of your loneliness, especially if there's a group of people around you." I didn't know it, but "group" was a trigger word, because we exist between lives in soul groups - "cluster groups" we call them. Her face lit up. She got tears in her eyes and pointed to my office wall and said, "I see them all."

I was thinking "Is she seeing them in this life? In a past life?" "Where are we?" I asked. "Oh," she said, **"We're in the spirit world. I'm seeing all my soul companions, they're wonderful,"** and she began describing them.

I probed more, took a lot of notes, and had a recording of the session. I found none of her soul companions in her life today and she was lonely because of it. After she left, I said to myself *This can't be happening to me*.

I'm the world's worst cynic, skeptic, and past lives was enough of a jolt of cold water, and now this? I studied my notes and the tape for a long time, and then with other clients, I began exploring it more and more. Once I started, I couldn't stop.

A TYPICAL SESSION

Can you walk us through a typical Life between Life session?

People come in because there may be a relative who recently died, or emotional trauma from losing a child. **This work is not to supplant therapy they should receive from a licensed trained professional; it's intended to provide them with answers about their inner being.**

One of the things clients don't understand until they experience it, is that there is a dual nature to all of us. We have our brain ego if you will, and we have a soul ego, and when they are combined it creates one personality and one lifetime.

The first hour, we pick a couple of childhood memories to get a sense of them recalling events earlier in this life, to prepare them to answer questions on a deeper level. Then we take them into their most immediate past life, because it's their most recent experience. It's very brief as it's not intended to be a discourse on past lives.

There are a number of past life therapists that don't have a clue about Life between Lives therapies - they think it's grayish 'limbo' that has no significance. **But we then cross from the death experience into the spirit world, into the afterlife; it's an interesting and exciting time for the client because they begin to really see their soul.**

Friends, relatives or their spirit guide, usually both, come to greet them - when a client sees their immortal teacher for the first time they're usually blown out of their minds. Some religious people think they see Jesus or Buddha or Mohammad coming towards them, but they quickly realize, "Oh, no, no, no… this is my personal teacher who's been with me since I was created as a soul."

From there, we move to interesting aspects of the spirit world, perhaps soul groups which range from 3 to 25 souls, the average client has about 15. These are all friends, relatives, spouses, dear friends in this life and some clients are shocked by who's there. There are other soul groups, nearby affiliated souls, that may play an important part in certain lives. There are reasons for that, and we try to explore it.

From there, they typically go in front of a group of wise beings - some call them "The Elders" or "The Wisdom Makers" - wise beings who are a step or two above their guides. These are non-incarnating beings, they're about as close to God as we get, and there's usually a very interesting discourse. They may ask the patient **"How do you think you did in your last life?"** They're very gentle people.

An interesting thing happens when they're ready to return in the next incarnation; **there's a life and body selection library where people choose different kinds of bodies and**

who they think they can work best with. Their elders and guides have a hand in their selection before they come forward into the next life. It's a fascinating process.

What's key is there's such order and discipline there and yet it's a very compassionate loving relationship. It isn't one that involves the kinds of things we see on Earth with a hierarchy of beings who lord over you and engender fear. **There is infinite forgiveness and understanding there. We all make mistakes, some of them terrible, and that's all forgiven once we cross over.**

When the clients wake up after one of these long sessions, some of them are crying and some of them are laughing, some of them can't talk - and generally there's just this "Wow. I can't believe it." Trying to process what's happened.

AFTERLIFE CLASSROOMS AND THE COUNCIL OF ELDERS

I've spoken with a few people who've referred to their own recurring dreams of being in a classroom somewhere in the Universe, some working with or without energy. Also, I'd like to know more about "The Elders."

We get flashbacks from time to time that break through that amnesiac block, folks who've had no LBL experiences, and just ordinary people that don't know about our work. Suddenly they're in a classroom in their dreams and they think "Hmm. That's a strange image; where's that coming from?" Most of us between lives spend time in a spiritual classroom. They are usually described as buildings, a library, or the place where they meet their council looks like a beautiful domed structure and in some cases a temple.

Of course, there aren't buildings in the ethereal space between lives, but people free-associate or have flashbacks of buildings; "I'm in a classroom, I have people around me that I know, there's a teacher…"

Essentially, we're given instruction by a Specialist Soul in areas we may have a talent or affinity for. They may be areas we'll specialize in after our incarnations are over - when we will be helping others. **I often hear about an energy creating class where they're working with raw energy to create certain things. I have the theory a lot of what we see on Earth in terms of plants and animals and geographies have been created by groups of advanced souls.**

When we visit the Elders, we talk about our lessons and what we might do differently in the future. We're not standing before God or a Creator or a Source - But people describe feeling kind of a God-like presence at these meetings. **It's hard for people to describe it; I need to speak to someone who's not incarnating anymore to give me answers to that sort of thing. Once in a while I got a highly advanced client who was in their last series of incarnations, who'd open the door a little bit, and it's beautiful to listen to.**

What kinds of questions would you like to know the answers to from this work?

When I get an advanced client in my chair, I feel sorry for them because I'm a relentless inquisitor. I've asked the question "What does it all mean?" with certain advanced clients. One thing I've learned is that we are only one of many universes. I've been able to hear about nine or ten dimensions, either parallel universes or universes that overlap in timelines, through patients. (He later told me that he'd visited as many as 27 in his work.)

Once you leave Earth, of course, you're not in linear time anymore, you're in what we call 'now time' - which is past, present and future... that's the best I can do on the question about creation - I wish I could tell you more.

QUANTUM PHYSICS AND THE AFTERLIFE

What do you think about the concept that photographs may be captured time?

It feeds into what we know about quantum physics - the Cherokee Indians believe no event in time is ever lost. I think from what I have discovered, nothing is ever lost; every moment of time represents particles of energy. It's like a movie that's being shown. That frame is there forever and can be recalled in the spirit world. Souls are able to go back to any event in any past life and review it completely.

This is one of things we do that is so valuable. When they're in the spirit world, in a library or a classroom, they're able to recall everything from their past; nothing ever dies and when you have past, present and future all conjoined into "now time" think of the advantage that brings to studying and reviewing what you've done and how you can make it better.

There are possibilities and probabilities in the time continuum and there have been wonderful books about parallel universes, the **"Holographic Universe" by Michael Talbot for example.**

It's very much in synch with reports we get from clients who've never read the books, so I feel the knowledge we're gaining now is greater than it's ever been about our inner being and the forces behind our creation.

Why hasn't this information been available earlier in our history?

I think there are a couple of reasons. We've never been so over-populated in history, with so many of us running in so many directions. Second, I think it's the pervasive use of drugs which has even reached our elementary schools - when someone is taking drugs to "escape from reality" it shuts down the soul. **And maybe the powers that be decided it's time to loosen up this amnesia bloc we all have when we come into this world so we're able to gain information that perhaps earlier was not really available."**[26]

*****

When Michael passed away, I wondered what it was like for him on the flipside but had not endeavored to ask him any questions about it. So imagine my chagrin when one day Jennifer said, *"He's over your shoulder."*

He had some specific messages to his friends at his Institute, including a joke about someone getting their hair cut too short. He had a specific message for Scott De Tamble, who he helped train to become a hypnotherapist. The messages were specific and geared to the person they were meant for.

---

[26] Excerpted from "Flipside: A Tourist's Guide on How to Navigate the Afterlife" by Richard Martini. Homina Publishing 2011. All Rights Reserved. Not to be reproduced without written permission.

I asked him what he was up to, what he was doing "now." He said, "I'm continuing my research into *noetic science*."[27] I had heard the term before, but neither Jennifer and I were familiar with it. I looked it up after our conversation.

So, Michael says he is continuing his research into how to communicate with the flipside. **But as he puts it, not research into how we can communicate with the flipside, but he's "taking notes on how to help people over there communicate with people over here."**

As I left after filming this encounter, I noticed somehow the word "Mnemonic" had shown up on my cellphone. It could have spontaneously appeared there, but I wasn't familiar with the term. (It's a form of memorizing things; like musical scales. "Every good boy does fine") That led me to research the goddess Mnemosyne, who was much more popular in the Greek era, when every play began with a prayer to the "Goddess of Memory" so the actors could remember their lines. Further, she was the person responsible for giving the dead a drink that made them remember all of their past lives. She administered another drink just prior to incarnation that would make them forget all their past lives.

Just another one of those odd things that happens in this research. That when we come here we take that drink of

---

[27] "The Institute of Noetic Sciences (IONS) is an American non-profit parapsychological research institute. It was co-founded in 1973 by former astronaut Edgar Mitchell, along with investor Paul N. Temple, and others interested in purported paranormal phenomena, in order to encourage and conduct research on noetic theory and human potentials. The Institute conducts research on ... survival of consciousness after bodily death." (Wikipedia)

"forget-me-Juice" (as Scott De Tamble calls it) where we don't have access to our previous information.

*****

Jennifer: Morton just showed up over your shoulder.

Rich: Who?

The guy you wrote the book about. You know.

I know Bob Morton. But he's alive. Oh. You mean Michael Newton? Really? How's he doing?

He's telling me that he came to visit you in a dream. He's showing me that he's taking notes.

> (Note: **I forgot about the dream, but later my wife reminded me that after he passed, I told her he'd visited me in a dream.** *Ding!*)

So you're taking notes on how to make it easier to communicate from over there to here, or from over here to there?

From where I am. He's taking notes from there, as to help people here… to be able to communicate here… it's to help everyone here, work with their conscious mind. He showed me, like a veil, lifting.

Is your work helping them communicate better to us over here? Is that what you're saying? Your life's work?

Yes. He's talking *there*, "Because we have everything here," he says.

He's helping them to have the ability to communicate with us?

Right.

On an energetic level?

"Yes. A matching level."

Any messages to your friends at the Institute?

He's kidding around. He's saying "To allow them to break off and to be okay with it. They don't need to have it (his methodology be) uniform..." Does that make sense?

Who should I express that too?

I asked him "Is it okay for them to break off?" He said, "Not unless they have an underlying thread of... holding each other together, but yet having your own uniqueness within it." Like not having that same systematic method, (but) just having an underlying thread. **He showed me the heart.** "That will influence way more people."

Let me paraphrase; "In terms of practicing the kind of deep hypnosis therapy he taught, he's saying the underlying thread needs to stay there and be connected to the heart, but individuals should be allowed to find it in their own way or to be able to branch out into their own methodology? Something like that?"

"Yes. To be able to be themselves." He says he had too much control about it.

I'm not sure that will resonate with his Institute, but I'll pass it along. So did you show up today to tell us that?

He says "No, I'm here because I'm taking notes."

On our conversation?

"I'm in communication mode. Yes. It's like noetic science but from the other side."

> (Note: "The Institute of Noetic Sciences describes noetic science as "how beliefs, thoughts, and intentions affect the physical world." This is not a term or concept that Jennifer or I are familiar with.)

I'm going on George Noory's show this weekend "Beyond Belief."[28] I'm sure your name will come up. Anything you want me to pass along?

"Tell Richard that everything he's set out to do; he's done, and then some - he's surpassed what he planned or signed up for... and beyond that."

Oh. (Flattered, trying to think of something funny, like "will I get an Oscar for that?") Will I get a lottery number soon?

"What good would that do?"

I understand. (Jennifer laughs) Let's ask Michael about that dream he mentioned. Remind me what was it that we talked about in my dream?

> (Note: When I told my wife Sherry about this conversation, she reminded me that the night after he died, I had a conversation with Michael. I asked him *"So how is the afterlife, is it as you pictured it?"* He said it was "different." I told me wife that Jennifer said that Michael told me I had a dream about him, and she said **"Remember? You said you spoke to him."**)

---

[28] https://www.gaia.com/video/hacking-afterlife-richard-martini

Or is there anything you want me to say on the talk show when your name comes up?

(Tell them) **"Everybody can speak to the other side. And that no one does not -** *not have the capability* **to do so. Everyone should start, they should start bringing them in closer." He showed me like both of these dimensions, of which there are a gazillion, but he showed me the dimensions of it -- being like at a dinner table where you're translucent to each other... yet you still have the energy of other people** (that are) **with you.**

An example might be; at Thanksgiving, add empty chairs to your table, toast or speak of those who aren't there?

"Yes!" (Jennifer aside) He just gave the best "Yes!"

A little bit like "Elijah and the Jewish tradition?" Put out a chair in case Elijah shows up?

"Yes."

All right. (Shaking my head.) A visit by Michael, wow.

Jennifer: (aside) Prince showed up at the end.

> (Note: Prince showed up at this same restaurant a few months prior, during another lunch. That conversation I filmed and included in *"Hacking the Afterlife."* We were just about to leave, but I said, "We can't not speak to Prince!")

Let's talk to him. Hello Mr. Prince Rogers Nelson. Does Prince have anything he wants to say on the "Beyond Belief" show?

Tell him that it's a "sound note..." he showed me the matrix... tell him, "It's a *sound* note."

> (Note: Funny word play as well. A musician giving us a "sound note." It's a note, just the way Michael was taking notes, but it's also a musical note, and a spiritual one as well.)

What's that mean?

I don't know. Hang on. "It's not how you look, (*I think he's referring to me worrying how I "looked on the show" which I did not express to Jennifer but was on my mind*) it's not what you say, (*it's not the content of what I'm saying on the show*) it's how you vibrate in your awareness. Awareness of one another."

(After a pause) "In your awareness of the accumulation." So like, he's showing me that in your awareness, it's a note... – so if your frequency is clear, that's how you attract someone. Because when you're in the consciousness of the higher level, where there is no hierarchy... and if you're bouncing (broadcasting) on a certain level, then that gets through with more potency.

When you're bouncing on a lower level, its fragmented. If it's fragmented, you're not able to connect, which logically, you can't connect." He's showing me "You don't connect well when you're out of mode of vibration -- but when you're not afraid of vibration, you're able to then send it out and then receive that higher vibration..."

A bit like we were saying earlier, when you strike a chord, all the guitars in a room start to vibrate at that same tone. You hit a note and all the guitars resonate on that same string?

"Yes."

So, the idea being not higher or lower, but stronger?

"But not all the same – *high* **frequencies can sound low." He showed me the song "Every rose has its thorns."**[29]

Higher -- meaning the place they're coming from?

Right. "You can… but if you have a higher (stronger) **frequency, you'll still connect with the people that will come. It's a matrix."**

My question for you Prince, since we last spoke in this same restaurant two months ago; what does that feel like to you in terms of time, comparatively?

"A millisecond – even less than that…" He just told me, "It's continuous." So like he was here and it's a continuous dialog. It's a continuous "dialog with God." He just showed me a goddess, but he's kidding around with that. (looks at her watch) I gotta go.

Prince, thanks for stopping by, we'll have to get back to you!

*****

---

[29] Every rose has it's thorn, Just like every night has it's dawn, Just like every cowboy sings his sad, sad song, Every rose has it's thorn..." by Miley Cyrus

CHAPTER FIVE:
MORTON'S ADVICE

"Faster, Smarter, More Efficient."

I passed along Michael's words of advice to some folks who worked with him in the Newton Institute. One said, "Keep up the conversation, no matter what." Another said, **"That doesn't sound like him at all. I don't know *who* you're talking to, but it doesn't sound like the Michael I knew."**

I try to point out that what we sound like "back home" is different than we sound "over here" "on stage" or "in the fish tank." It would be illogical for us to sound *just like* we did when we were here when you factor in all that is left onstage, or in the fish tank.

I can say I'm petty up on Michael's curriculum vitae: his three books, "Journey of Souls," "Destiny of Souls," and "Life Between Lives." I've interviewed a number of the people who appeared in "Memories of the Afterlife" which he edited.

I interviewed him for three hours, spent an hour with his dear wife Peggy Jene as well.

Subsequently I've tracked down his fraternity photos from the University of Arizona where he was a Liberal Arts major and a member of Theta Chi. I have a copy of his dissertation from the University that granted him a Doctor of Philosophy in the 1980's. (As directed to by Jennifer as to where to find it.)

But even then, I'm not claiming we're speaking to Michael Newton.

The flipside is so complex, and what appears to be finite is a partially a reflection of the person asking questions, and the person who is responding to them. It's like someone being asked questions by three people; a colleague, a stranger, and a child. Each answer is tailored to the person asking the question. The colleague might get a response that is filled with references to higher knowledge, the stranger might get an answered tailored to their ability to comprehend, and the child might get a pat on the head and a tickle.

Recently, a friend on Facebook was posting something about speaking to a guide on his "council" (a term Newton used often) and he asked his counselor what it felt like for him to be answering his questions. The council member replied, *"Like an old man talking to a little baby."* So there's that as well – Michael (or some facsimile of him) may be tailoring his answers.

Plus, when we explore the idea of person "experiencing the flipside," they're accessing many forms of communication – including visuals, senses, pulling information from various time frames, past lives, etc. They communicate differently over there entirely. When that's all factored in, it explains why this research is filled with all kinds of conjecture – claims of apocalyptic visions of the future – or hierarchies in the afterlife or claims of "channelers" predicting the future.

But we tend to consider the people being "channeled" as being omniscient. They can relate their experiences, and they may be vast – but they are based on their own path and journey. Just because they're off the planet doesn't make them all knowing. For example, I've had conversations with my "guide" – but he pointed out to me that his experiences are a combination of both his and mine – but not everyone else's. We can't be in someone else's shoes, unless... we are in someone else's shoes (or in their soul group.)

And a note to what people claim when hearing from "older wiser souls." What I consistently hear is "There is no hierarchy over here." Old souls consider young souls equally important, and vice versa. They may have more experience, but that doesn't mean they necessarily have more insight.

As Scott De Tamble puts it; "I've met all kinds of guides and higher elevated beings during my sessions. They appear as wizards, wearing robes and outfits that speak of great sages and people who have great respect for knowledge. But when I ask them to present themselves as *they see themselves*, they always speak of a ball of light." In other words, even the greatest sages are *blobs of light* trying to navigate their version of reality.

In that vein, we are all "blobs of light." The idea that I believe that I'm "talking to a blob of light" who once identified in this lifetime as "Mike Duff Newton" "Theta Chi, Class of 1953" doesn't negate anything he has to say. Rather, as said in the introduction; "If what this blob of light has to say about the journey we're all on, and it resonates with you, *then take it with a grain of salt."*

As Jennifer's father so aptly advised her; "Your job is not to prove that there is an afterlife. It's to give testimony and report as truthfully as you can what you are hearing." **And if that helps someone else on their path or journey, then we've done our job.**

*****

Rich: I'm going to ask you some goofy questions today.

Jennifer: As opposed to? (laughs.)

So you mentioned that our buddy Morton showed up earlier.

He says "Condense, first thing is to condense. You're supposed to teach the teachers how to simplify, you have a great understand of how to simplify things." I'm getting the word "process" from him. And he's making fun of me because I keep forgetting his name.

Michael Newton.

He said "Morton." I had said "Norton" in my mind, and he corrected me. So as before, when we were discussing how to simplify communication, he said he was "taking notes" over there – notes on how to converse over here – he just showed me Steve Jobs.

For what reason?

To simplify communication and because I've asked Steve Jobs to make it better over there with people who've known him; I've had some clients who knew him well, and I took it very much personally when he passed. That being said, asking him to make it better or easier for us to communicate the other way around.

What I got was, "Each person has their own cellphone number, each frequency is very unique to the person you're calling. **So when you open your heart up, you can communicate with people who have your frequency."**

Oh... Michael showed up again... he's saying, "This conversation helps people connect faster – **it's a frequency, so you can teach how to make faster, smarter and more efficient."**

Let's ask Steve a question. When you passed away you reportedly said "Oh wow, oh wow, oh wow..." What was in your field of reference when you said that?

He showed me that he saw the universe... like the pale blue dot photo of the earth; he saw the entire universe that way and the magic of how connected everything is, including butterflies and the people and lights, how it's all connected.

Could you put that visual into Jennifer's pov?

It feels like being able to *send* at the same time as you *receive*... you're able to see everything – be connected to everything; he's showing me living things like the butterflies... (She lifts her Apple wrist watch and a butterfly appears)

You mean the energy of a butterfly? Or actual butterflies?

Like, it's the cosmic way we transform; that it was like he was a caterpillar first while being in human form and how we're in the infancy stage while we're here, and (then) he

felt like he was in a cocoon (chrysalis) **here and turned into a butterfly, in order to cross over.**

Wow. Okay, thanks Steven; I know when I did a session with a friend who worked for both you and Bill Gates.

"She was a pain in the ass!" he said, but kiddingly... He added "She was a "smart pain in the ass."

I've known her since high school.

> (Note: Her LBL appears in "It's a Wonderful Afterlife." Very smart person, well respected in her field of science. But funny for him to make this comment – Jennifer has no way of knowing her acerbic delivery. She was convinced that she wouldn't go anywhere during her deep hypnosis session – and it took about 5 hours before she did. But once she did, it all came to her as a download.)

"She was a protector of both in some way, she did her job well. She stirred the pot, stirred them up to get them to do things or think differently." *Does that make sense?*

It does. When she did a session with our pal Scott De Tamble at some point I asked about her old boss Steve Jobs.[30]

He showed me he stopped by, **kind of snuck through the session.** At first, he appeared as something or someone else, then appeared as himself.

---

[30] Scott Fitzgerald De Tamble, C. Ht., C. M. T., is a Clinical Hypnotherapist, specializing in Past Life Regression and Life Between Lives Spiritual Regression. lightbetweenlives.com

> (Note: This is accurate with regard to the session that I filmed. She "saw him" slip past, and Scott asked her to bring him back and questioned him.)

I appreciate that. I'd like to skip back to Michael.

Michael says, "He's in great company."

*The last time we met, as I left the restaurant, and we were talking about memory, the word **Mnemonic** appeared on my phone. I figured it was related to our conversation.*

It was him. Morton.

> (Note: We had been talking about "memory" and how to access our memories on the flipside, and when I got to my car, the word mnemonic was written as if I had typed it out. I've never written the word mnemonic, prior to this book. It's possible that the word was "auto suggested" by my cellphone, just never seen it before.)

When I looked up mnemonic, I found that the Goddess of memory, Mnemosyne.[31] As the myth goes, she's in charge of people remembering their previous lives once they get to the Flipside. I wondered if you put that on my cell phone, so I would look it up.

---

[31] Mnemosyne; "The goddess of memory" would assist actors doing Greek plays that sometimes lasted days. Every performance began with a prayer to her. She's also the person who gives souls a drink of the river Lethe when they incarnate so they "forget previous lifetimes," - but when they cross over, she gives a drink from her river, which allows souls to remember "all their previous lifetimes." In terms of this research; a precise metaphor for the process.

He did. He says, "You're exhausting; it's hard to work with you! But he wants you to help those trained by him to streamline the process."

Very hard for me to suggest that to the folks who run the Institute.

He's helping you.

Thanks. Okay let's shift to Jennifer's dad Jim, the only Bishop in the room.

> (Note: Jennifer's father was a Mormon bishop who passed a few months prior to this conversation.)

"Thank you," he says.

I appreciate you stopping by, Jim.

(Jennifer turns red, can't speak.) He's laughing because I have a lump in my throat... He says, "I wanted you to know how much I love you and I hope it's not just one sided." That was something my grandfather would say...

Can you take a hold of your dad's hand and send him some radiating love, so he can feel it?

He always loved driving fast, he always takes me into the ether when he appears. I feel like he's taking me for a ride.

Can you do that now?

He says he's learning (to navigate the afterlife). Shows me falling on his elbow... so funny... "It's endless," he says. "The universe is endless."

What's the best way to connect to someone no longer on the planet?

"Through the heart; putting the awareness of your loved ones in the heart." They're all laughing. I just asked, "You mean like a cell phone?" They said "Yes, your heart's a cellphone. You have to put your intentions into your heart, that's your cell phone. It's how you connect with them."

Anyone else in the room who wants to come forward?

Prince. He's saying, (communication) **"It's like the frequencies of music. Your heart is like a guitar, in that it has strings, and those strings vibrate, and they call or connect you to the others who are connected to you..."** that awareness because it takes you places.

"Music reminds you of things you've done in your past, memories, music and words mean something to your heart. The strings are the strands of the matrix, like a guitar that connects you (plugs you in) **to the matrix."**

Listening to music is a way of connecting to your heart? A way to connect to a loved one no longer on the planet would be to play their favorite song?

"Yes. And ask them questions," he said.

Mr. Nelson, Prince Rogers, everyone's excited your music is coming out since you've crossed over; people are playing it everywhere. That must be a kick for you.

He says "It connects him to everyone. When somebody sends his music to others." He's showing me - you know how they show a stadium with all the lights? He showed me that it's like that for him - everyone playing his music and they all connect back.

I know we've talked about the meaning of Purple Rain...

He's saying, "It was seductive phrase."

But I wanted to mention how in Newton's work, he found that people connected to certain colors on the spectrum...

He's saying Michael already explained that to him.

Michael heard from people under hypnosis that the color purple related to older souls – he reported that the younger souls radiated in a white or yellow light, the start of the visible spectrum, and the older souls that he met, when asked "If you looked in a mirror, what color of light would you see?" And the older ones would radiate in that purple end of the spectrum.

Prince is saying, "It was (just) his favorite color and he looked good in it!"

Okay. Let me ask you the same – if you looked yourself in a mirror what color would you see?

He said, "Red." (Jennifer blushed, said "he's flirting with me.") "He's more grounded into it and so that's the color he's at now; red."

Okay, we've got to go, class, thanks to everyone for showing up. Jennifer is not quite my cell phone, but my Dixie-Cup-On-a-String connection to the flipside.

*****

A friend recently asked me *"Do you actually believe you're talking to these people?"* I said "I try to leave the concept of *belief* out of my work. I have the *experience* of talking to someone who makes me feel as if I'm talking to these people, and I ask my questions accordingly." Once we have an "experience" of talking to someone no longer on the planet our paradigm shifts. As mind did when my dad "visited" me the night he passed with the names of his friends on the flipside I had never heard of, but my mother confirmed were his "friends who died in World War II." Or when James Van Praagh quoted Luana as saying I had a photograph on my refrigerator that was the "essence of our relationship" – a detail no one but me could know.

I've dropped the idea of "belief" and focused on the content of what they're saying. I have no idea if it's actually Prince talking about frequencies and music. But being a musician and someone who used to sell stereo equipment, I know about tuning, frequencies that are limited, blocked or filtered, or how and when they resonate with each other. If it is or isn't Prince, the metaphors he's using, the concepts he's offering, are equally worth noting.

Besides, whoever it is that's coming through is *really entertaining.*

Luana reaching beyond the veil with her gaze.

CHAPTER SIX:

HARVARD TO OXFORD AND BACK with JULIAN THE PHD

"To teach you."

Julian Baird was my professor in Boston University. He was in charge of the Humanities program at DGE – the "Division of General Education." It was a "pre-law" program designed for advanced students at the University. Julian was the first person I met at BU and he convinced me to attend. He had PhDs from Oxford and Harvard. I thought *"Really? I can take classes with this guy? Where do I sign up?"*

Julian grew up in a small town in Texas, was from a poor family, but earned a scholarship to Harvard. After Harvard he earned a scholarship to Oxford. After Oxford he earned another scholarship to get his PhD at Harvard, then taught there. He went to Boston University to teach, where I met him, then left the University after it took a political turn to the right in the mid-80's. He wandered into an art gallery (Trees Gallery in Orleans, MA) on the Cape and bought it. He became a patron and curator of Cape Cod art and artists and became very wealthy doing so.

I loved him as a friend and teacher. After college, I used to send him postcards from around the world whenever I traveled. Imagine my shock when I get a postcard returned and someone had scrawled "Julian has died of brain cancer. Stop sending these cards." I mourned the loss of my friend and teacher.

Then some 20 years later, I was thinking of him and wondered if someone had a tribute page for him on Facebook. I was startled to see that not only was still alive but thriving. I wrote to him and he said that he suspected it was his "very angry ex-wife" who had sent me that postcard in the midst of their ugly divorce. He then brought me up to date on his life. He was happily married and living on Cape Cod.

I felt I had been robbed of this man's intellect and humor for a third of my life. *What a cruel thing to do*!

But after a few years of promises for me to come and visit, Julian reported the doctors advised him his leukemia was advanced; he had not much longer to live. He had decided instead of having a large funeral, he would throw a wake of sorts – an all-expense-paid party for his friends. I offered to film the event for him.

It's on YouTube. *"A Portrait of Julian Baird"* (after the Joyce title "Portrait of the Artist as a Young Man" which he introduced me to.)[32]

I interviewed many of the artists whose careers he'd help flourish, and then spent a day at his home learning about his own journey. We touched on the topic of the afterlife, and he was adamant that *there wasn't any.* Besides, he said, **"I'm more interested in being alive rather than what happens when I'm not."**

I quote Julian often. When I disagree with someone's point, I repeat what he used to say in class; **"I'd agree with you but then we'd both be wrong."** I know that his friends back east will find this direct interview with him odd to say the least.

The point isn't to focus on any one detail. It's that you're going to hear dozens of these interviews in the course of these books, there are many details that I can verify, that are shown to be accurate. There will be details that don't make any sense; imagine seeing a television for the first time and trying to make sense of what we're seeing. It's a lot of images that may not make sense at first, but after some time or practice they begin to form a story.

In this case – this is just another story. I can verify certain details of what Julian says, and there are other details I cannot. (For example, I can't get anyone to tell me if Lady Gaga bought art from his gallery.) But when Jennifer "sees" Lady Gaga associated with Julian, it could mean that she went into the gallery years after he died, it could mean that she knows one of the artists associated with the gallery, it could

---

[32] "A Portrait of Julian Baird" https://youtu.be/xfUnLFkk5Uo

be that she's purchased art from one of the artists in the gallery.

In these accounts I include whatever information I can to help others verify what Jennifer is hearing or seeing. What I can verify during these sessions, I make a "note" of.

But in this case, this was a good friend who I lost due to someone else's vitriol – and now he's going to live on in my book at least. It's the least I can do to bring him back to life for the people who knew and loved him.

*****

Rich: (After lunch, I ask Jennifer:) Are they here, waiting?

Jennifer: They've been waiting. (She taps her wrist to indicate "we're late.")

I wanted to invite a guest speaker to join us today.

They already have him.

> (Note: Often, a day or so before our conversation I think of someone I would like to speak with in our "class." In this case, it was Julian.)

His first name is Julian. He was a professor at Boston University.

Did he die of a heart attack?

Could be, I'm not sure what his last day was like.

He had cancer.

Correct; leukemia.

He says, "He had it for a long time."

> (Note: This is correct as well. *Ding!* He was treated for leukemia for a number of years prior to his passing.)

He had a party for himself...

(Quickly) **Before he left.**

That's right.

> (Note: The invite read "I won't be here much longer, so instead of coming to my funeral, come to my wake." I interviewed many of his lifelong friends and people who's lives he had changed, and I made a speech as well.)

Julian, we're going to ask you the same questions we asked Harry Dean Stanton.

"I thought you would never ask," he says.

Who was there to greet you when you crossed over?

(Pause) **His mother.**

When she appeared, did you see her as older or younger?

He saw her in her early 60's. She feels like she was very prim and proper, like with bouffant hair...

> (Note: I found a photo of her, very prim and proper and with big hair.)

Julian, I interviewed you about the afterlife prior to your passing; you were adamant it it did not exist. At what point did you realize you were in the afterlife?

When he was hovering over his body.

What was that like?

It felt like a release. From pain... or... of all of it... (Jennifer asks Julian) "Was it a release of crossing over, or a release of your pain?" (a pause) He said, "All of it."

Let me ask you some questions about your journey or path. Are you currently aware of your previous lifetimes?

"I am."

So why did you choose this lifetime?

"To teach you."

(I laugh) *To teach many; you were a wonderful teacher.*

He's very diplomatic in his answers... he says... okay, hold on. I'm getting that he's smart, witty and funny. Very dry. (That's accurate) **Did he drink scotch?**

Not sure. There were a number of fine wines at his "wake" celebration... Julian, now that you have access from your past lives why did you choose this little town (Harlingen) in Texas?

I feel like you asked for him two days ago?

I did. (Two days earlier I thought about speaking to him during our session and called him aloud.) So tell us, what are you doing over there?

He's laughing. "Nothing. But everything."

> (Note: It sounds like one of the answers he would give while teaching Humanities at Boston University.

> He spoke often of understanding the macro in the microcosm. "No thing *is* nothing, and *nothing* is everything.")

So why did you choose this life of this young kid in East Texas?

When you said Texas, the other guy showed up. Bill.

> (Note: Our conversations with Bill Paxton are elsewhere in the book.)

Yes, Billy – both from Texas. Billy, this is my pal Julian; Julian, Billy.

(Jennifer listens.) Let's see if I got this straight... He says that **"The reason why he chose this lifetime was to learn how to not come back."**

I think I get it. "To learn how to not come back." Julian was a deep guy, a profound thinker.

> (Note: According to these reports, we learn from each lifetime, and after many lifetimes, we eventually "graduate" to a higher level, a "non-reincarnating person" who might serve in some other capacity "back home" – counselor, guide, etc. But also, people claim that we can opt out of a future life choice, we can say "no thanks" to a future life suggestion by our loved ones and guides.)

He's showing me a portrait of that psychologist... Jung?

Julian, why are you showing her Carl Jung? Are you referring to his theories or ideas about the unconscious?

He said, "It was the only time that he (Julian) **questioned the afterlife... going through Carl Jung's work."**

Until he met me of course. Just kidding. Here you were, this young boy in Harlingen. As I remember it you won some contest and they invited you to Harvard.

"Twice," he said.

> (Note: ***Ding!*** This is an example of **new information.** Jennifer knows nothing about Julian, but I know that he was invited to Harvard twice on scholarships, first as an undergraduate student, then he was invited to Oxford on a scholarship, and afterwards invited back to Harvard on a scholarship to earn his PhD and to teach. No one would ever reply to "You went to Harvard" and they reply "twice." *Does not make sense.*)

Rich: Yes. Twice he went to Harvard. That is correct. So when you got to Harvard in the 1950's you were studying ancient English lit – studying Beowulf in its original Old English language.

Jennifer: He just gave me the chills... hold on a second. He says, "He went to Harvard to see if they knew more than he did." He's very funny.

Did you have a previous lifetime where you spoke that ancient language, the language of Beowulf?

"Many."

You're aware of them now?

"Yeah."

They invited you to Harvard. Then you went to Oxford...

"Natural Selection." He says he "stayed longer than he wanted to."

You stayed longer in London? Why? Was it for the studying or something else?

He says, "For love."

Was that to meet your crazy wife who wrote me that evil postcard?

He's saying he had two wives...

Yes, that's correct. I'm referring to number one. She wrote me a postcard saying Julian was dead and for 20 years I mourned him. Then I found him on Facebook; he told me she had done that out of spite – so I missed out on 20 years of a beautiful friendship.

I saw "Facebook" as you were speaking, but then when you mentioned Harvard, I thought it was because of Zuckerberg.

Yes, he went to Harvard as well. After undergraduate work at Harvard, Julian went to Oxford they invited him back to Harvard on another scholarship.

> (Note: Julian recommended I transfer across the river my Junior year, wrote me a letter of recommendation to Harvard, but I wound up having my Junior Year in Rome instead. Much happier choice.)

I feel like that second time he came back, he taught.

Yes, correct. He got a PhD, then taught. Then he went to Boston University where I met him.

He just showed me that film *"Call Me By Your Name"* with the professor and a young son... the one that is dedicated to Bill Paxton... (to Julian) Why am I seeing art? Or paintings?

Because when Julian left Boston University, he went to Cape Cod where he walked into a gallery one day...

I see that as you're speaking. **I'm asking him "Why are you showing me art?" I was asking him "Were you doing art or doing writing?"**

Show her the gallery, Julian.

He fell in love, "Absolutely fell head over heels in love when he walked into that gallery." It felt so rich, he felt so enriched by being there.

Trees Place Gallery in Orleans, MA. He bought it.

No kidding?

He bought the gallery and then became this well-respected art dealer who sold art and became really successful doing it.

> (Note: As a teacher of Humanities, he spoke eloquently about art, about light, and as a gallery owner, he created a school of art about the light of Cape Cod and became quite successful at, earning a fortune in the process. He coined the term *"The New American Luminists."*)

"Best thing he ever did" he says.

When I filmed his wake, the party he had before he died, it was filled with famous Cape Cod artists who came to pay homage to him and spoke eloquently about him on camera.

Why is he showing me Lady Gaga?

I don't know... maybe she bought some art from the gallery.

He's showing me that she *has* gone into the gallery or bought art from those artists. She bought something now.

> (Note: Lady Gaga has reportedly built a home on Cape Cod, where she went in her youth. I don't know if she's made her way into Trees Gallery or or purchased art from the artists within, but it's a way of verifying what Jennifer is seeing.) [33]

That would be a way of validating what we're talking about. Let's return to our discussion as we talked about there being an afterlife. Julian, when you went back home – you reconnected with your higher consciousness. What was that experience like?

"Yeah, I did, but when I was here (on the planet)...." **He's saying, "It was like someone was knocking but no one was answering."**

But now you are aware of it; what's your observation (of the flipside)?

"It's like art or music." The visual he's showing me is like the way art or paint shows up in the matrix as frequencies, with all the different connections, with all the colors and vibrations and frequencies that go into (the act of) painting. "It's similar..." It's like that art gallery he

---

[33] Lady Gaga built a home recently in nearby Martha's Vineyard.) She's reportedly been purchasing artwork as well.
https://www.artspace.com/magazine/news_events/newsmaker/newsmaker_lady_gaga-51618

walked into. Like experiencing these eclectic portraits of humanity, these masterpieces of humans that are both here *and* there.

So how do you occupy your time now?

He just looked at Luana.

Why?

"Because she's my mentor."

Is this the first time that you've met Luana? Or have you met her before?

He said "No." He said, "Not the first time." Hold on. (Jennifer listens). He says he "Met her right after he crossed."

What was your impression of her when you met her?

He just looked up. He showed me all the white space beyond... "She's kind of a big deal."

So Luana, your pal Sandra Nicholson recently posted a clip of you from an episode of "One Step Beyond" recently that you both did in the 1960's, when you played "The Burning Girl."[34]

She just showed me lots of people smoking... back in that time...

I mentioned to Sandra how I used to tease you as "the Burning Girl" because you were someone who could start

---

[34] "The Burning Girl" https://youtu.be/WtxJB1-ud8k

fires with your wit when someone crossed you. I also noted how we spent most of our time laughing.

"It's the best therapy," Julian says. He's saying, "It's an anniversary."

Yes, it is. It's the same time of year that I made that film of your wake. Julian anything you want me to impart to your friends?

He says, **"Tell them not to *believe* in the afterlife... but do not discount how it arrives."**

What does that mean?

"It's a way for the non-conscious to give back one's light... for the unconscious to bring back one's light that dims when leaving the lifetime. And you don't have to believe that the afterlife exists, but for certain, you will, for sure, be excited that it does."

Which is kind of what Harry Dean Stanton told us.

(Jennifer aside) I told him "Thank you."

About how old does Julian appear to you?

He's about 50, wearing a sports jacket, khakis, has on a belt, like a button-down shirt and a cap with a feather in it...

Like a Robin Hood hat?

More like a British professor. In a fedora.

Julian, how do you create that fedora, so Jennifer can see it?

He says, "He materializes a memory."

How do you do that?

From what I (Jennifer) **have in my head.**

You're using a visual reference, like a holographic image in your head – and she's looking at that wave length and seeing the hat?

"As a hypothetical hat." He shows me that we all have multi-lifetime memories (of various pieces of clothing) **so he just maps it out** (for me).

So Jennifer can see it?

"We both participate" (in the construct).

Jennifer needs to help as well?

"Yes."

During a session, (hypnotherapist) Scott De Tamble asked me what color represented my dad, and before my eyes my father dissolved into light, and when I finished describing the quality of that light, he reanimated into my dad. I wondered, "Did I make that frequency adjustment or or did he?"

"Both. You both have to be open to receive it."

Julian, let's focus on the idea of shifting your focus in this plane so that a person or object disappears or dissolves. Can a person do that on the planet?

He's showing me Buddhist monks (that can).

I've heard those kinds of reports.

> (Note: There are some reports of Tibetan monks shape shifting, animating animals that have died,

many of them described in "The Six Yogas of Naropa." I'm familiar with these esoteric reports and have been to Tibet to the same places where they supposedly occurred.)

"It takes their awareness to be open to it." He's showing me that people that are around him, they put a shield around their awareness... like the example of seeing a penny appear in front of you.

(Note: The penny is not visible because the awareness of it is blocked – meaning the signals that normally indicate "penny on floor" are not functioning because of "created interference." But then when the penny "appears" (like in a sleight of hand trick) it's always been there, we just were not aware of it. This seems to explain how people "find" objects related to loved ones who have crossed over.)

Let me ask you about "dissolving." For example, a monk locks himself into a cave or a room, and a week later when they go in, they find only fingernails, hair and the robes – as if they somehow self-immolated, burned up or disappeared. They call it a "Rainbow death." How does that happen? Is it a matter of frequency?

"No, they dematerialize because they were never fully here in the first place."

How about you? Did you have a previous lifetime as a Buddhist monk?

He's showing me... Robert Thurman. Did they know each other?

I don't think so. But Robert was formerly a Buddhist monk... was he the same sect? Gelupka? They wear red and gold robes.

"Yes." He's saying he was, "But in this lifetime as a teacher, he chose a different route with words and art *in* life, instead of *escaping* life."

I remember when I first met you, you were a Zen Buddhist – and you were talking about it during class...

He just made a gesture (with his hand) **to show me "Blah Blah Blah..."**

Okay, I get that. It was my introduction to the concept. But what was that journey about with your first wife? (the crazy one.)

He said, **"She's not with me!"** They're all laughing...

Anything you want me to say to your family?

He said, **"Tell them I'm not dead."** He's laughing.

> (Note: I did. Not sure if they appreciated hearing it though, as they must think I'm nuts. Which is okay; perhaps I am.)

Did you like the film I made about you "A Portrait of Julian Baird?

"Very much. But It was too long."

> (Note: Another piece of **new information**. *Ding!* Jennifer has no way of knowing how long or short the film was. I edited Part One at 90 minutes; Part Two is over 2 1/2 hours.)

It was. But how and where do you edit someone you admire? You just don't want to miss anything.

He says, "Thank you, I know you put your heart and soul in it."

At some point I gave up editing it... just posted the raw footage.

Jennifer: **He said that** (as well).

Rich: I just didn't get around to finishing part two. Sorry.

"For a (portrait of a) **whole lifetime, it's pretty good,"** **he says.**

Well... Thanks.

He's showing me (Jennifer). He said, "Apparently you're having a portrait done right now." (She gestures to my camera aimed at her).

That's true. So is this the best way of communicating with people on the flipside?

He is showing me there's a list... he showed me like a long list... like a scroll... he's showing me a list that goes all the way out the door.

Of what? People we're going to be talking to in this fashion?

He said "No, they (the list) **are people who are learning** *how* **to talk to us. A lot of people don't realize they're talking to the other side." We're** (indicating me and Jennifer) **the only conscious ones doing it – and now they're learning what it is to talk to them.**

To communicate with the flipside and vice versa?

"That dual frequency – which is required from both sides."

Like the 11:11 dream Luana gave to my wife, Sherry.

> (Note: As noted; Luana showed the digital numbers 11:11 to my wife in a dream. She said, **"It's where the decimals are that we can connect."** Meaning we both have to "lean in" from either side, adjust our frequency in order to communicate.)

Julian said, "Just believe and you will get it." (Jennifer aside) **I asked him "A belief?" He said, "No. Get rid of belief and believe."**

"Get rid of belief (religious dogma) and just believe (in the afterlife)?"

"Believe in something greater than yourself."

Thank you. What about your father, Jennifer? Does your dad Jim want to add anything to this discussion?

Okay. Hold on. He's showing me that he put that thought in your head (to ask about him). **That was interesting.**

> (Note: Jennifer's father had passed a year earlier and is a frequent visitor to our discussions since crossing over.)

What do you think of this trip that Jennifer is about to take, to go to the South Pacific to watch the lunar eclipse?

He said, "He made sure that I wouldn't miss it." (Note: Love of the moon was something Jennifer and her father shared through photos and other lunar events.)

Let me ask you a question about the moon. Can you visit there (while on the Flipside) and walk on the moon?

They're all laughing. I don't know why that's so funny.

I don't mean would you, but I mean, could you?

"Not really. They can go next to it..." He showed me like a barrier or shield...

A barrier between our reality and their reality?

(Jennifer taps her nose. Luana's way of saying "that's correct.")

Jim, there's an American flag on the moon, frozen. Can you transport your energy and go and stand next to that flag?

He laughs. He says, "The flag was stolen." He showed me a space ship taking off, the back of a space ship after stealing it. So funny!

Can we walk on the moon?

"No, but I can see how it was created."

How was it created?

He said "Through the intelligence of God – or source energy, and Jesus..."

Hang on. The creation of the moon was based on what?

"The blast – the Big Bang." Julian is coming back in to answer this question. **He's helping my dad... he's not helping my dad, because my dad is arguing (with him that) "he knows how to work with me..." okay.**

145

(Note: A funny exchange. "Hey! I know how to talk to my daughter!")

He said, "The moon is also a mind effect – "It's real," they said, "Yes, but if you don't know what a ship is - you wouldn't see the ship as it appeared on the horizon."

A philosophical point about perspective? Not sure if I'm following you.

"Everything is energy in the solar system." (Jennifer aside) I'm asking why they can't visit the moon etherically and the answer is "Because they have boundaries."

Let me ask you this Jim. If I can ask you to sit next to Jennifer, can you do that?

"Yes."

If I suggested you manifest yourself standing under the Eiffel tower, can you do that as well?

"Sure, but I don't want to." Hold on... The reason why he didn't want to go there (to the Eiffel tower), is because he knows the frequencies of where I am; that frequency is easier to connect with. He never went there. That's why... because he doesn't have the frequency of the Eiffel tower experience, he can't go there. They go to the frequency of us.

So if you knew someone who'd been to the moon, could you ride their frequency of their memory to go there?

"Yes."

And in general, you can't go to places that you haven't been?

"Yes."

Can someone travel to Mars?

"We all have (been there), that was the starting point."

> (Note: I've heard this before, some people under deep hypnosis claim that we had originally decided upon Mars as a place to incarnate, but for technical reasons, the life experiments that began there did not take, or did not remain. (Scientists tell us that the magnetic field of Mars is not conducive to life, but that there is some evidence that water has been there in the past.) For whatever reason, Mars was reportedly a "failed experiment" which then "worked" on Earth.
>
> I have no way of proving or disproving their claims, but I would not be surprised if at some point we find evidence of rudimentary life forms on Mars. "Coming from a place" doesn't necessarily mean we were there in human form, because life takes a variety of forms. It may have been a more rudimentary form of "sentient life.")

Rich: But those who haven't been to the moon can't get back there?

Jennifer: He's showing me that the closest he can get to the moon itself, is through me watching it in the South Pacific (as she's about to do.)

Julian, question for you; have we had many "Big Bangs" or just one?

"Many."

(Note: This follows the report in Hindu philosophy that we are living in an aeon – a "kalpa" and that there have been many kalpas. That the universe has expanded and contracted many times before, that there have been many iterations of planets or Earths, that energy doesn't end, it transforms, and we've lived lifetimes in this universe many other times. Hard to wrap a mind around, but I was trying to see how he would answer the question.)

So moons have formed and unformed, Earths have formed and unformed, so the idea that Jesus and/or God are involved in their creation is a kind of super-extension of the process, but they're not directly involved. Or are they?

"Right; it's a by product of the process..."

And as we've heard (before in previous conversations) that Jesus is just one of many avatars that has been on the planet that would be identified as being close to source, is that correct?

(Jennifer taps her nose to say "correct.")

I just wanted to clarify that concept – the part with Jesus, God and the moon in the same sentence... that it's a complex process.

(Note: Like anyone, I go into a brain freeze when someone speaks of "the intelligence of God." Hence why I asked these follow up cosmology questions.)

Well, thanks for showing up Julian. Paxton, sorry we didn't get to you.

He's there.

Anything you want to say?

A salute and a kiss. (She does it with two fingers on her lips.)

How about my pal Billy Meyer? It's around his birthday today. (Billy passed a number of years prior, actually appeared to Jennifer while I was interviewing her on camera for German television. She let me know that he was visiting and moments later got a text telling me of his passing.)

He said, "Thank you for reaching out to his family, it was helpful."

And how about our friend, Craig Ottinger? He's a mutual friend of ours, kind of shy, doesn't like to speak up... died some years ago.

He's got a bunch of motorcycles... he has a collection (over there.)

> (Note: Craig has shown up in the past, I can't remember if I told her he raced motorcycles, but at this point, I don't bother checking the record on these kinds of details. *Of course* he would be on the flipside enjoying motorcycles. He had the coolest ones when I knew him.)

I'm sure he does. Anything about the dream last night I had about my father and architecture?

Jennifer asks: "Were you trying to show Richard... it was infinite?" Your father says "No, I was trying to show him not to think small. There are limitless possibilities."

As an architect, I imagine you're designing things over there.

He laughed, said **"He's too busy helping you."**

Anything else?

Paxton wants to say, **"Tell everybody not to discount who is around. Loved ones."**

You mean loved ones who have passed away?

"Yes. Don't discount the loved ones who they sense are around. Ask questions, like you do, Rich."

And how do they know its their loved ones when they get the answer?

"In their heart, they'll know. Ask for numbers, ask for signs, they'll put their awareness towards it."

Okay class, Jennifer has to go; catch you all on the flipside.

Luana and me hamming it up

CHAPTER SEVEN:
TOM WILBURY
"Backstage Pass"

A mirror in a mirror in Rockefeller Plaza with Luana

In general, we've found that this process is easiest when either Jennifer or I knew the person that we bring forth to interview. It's almost as if "our frequency" is familiar with "their frequency" so inviting them to come and chat with us is easier to do.

Needless to say, whenever we think of someone we knew, we are accessing the files that we have for that person. Those files contain frequency information – because everything we see, hear, touch, feel – is a wavelength that comes to us, and our mind translates that wavelength into information or a memory. When you remember something you're accessing that frequency of the memory.

So even when we think of a loved one who is no longer on the planet, we get a mental image of them, or we may get many senses involved; hearing their voice, smelling a perfume, remembering a meal, etc. Their ability to "*ping*" or get our mind to remember them is a matter of activating a frequency or "sending a signal" to get us to recollect our memory of them.

Apparently, it works the same way with dreams. It's reportedly easier for them to "enter our dreams" because we aren't blocking frequencies while we're asleep, we're more open to other information.

In the between life studies of Michael Newton, many discussed the process of how once they were no longer on the planet, they went about "implanting" a dream into someone's sleep. They claimed that they chose a neutral setting, so as not to freak out their loved one, and often said or did something in the dream that they could remember when they woke up. (Note: The same way that Paul McCartney's mother Mary appeared to him in a dream and said *"Let it be"* – which he turned into a song.) All memory is frequency, all visitations from people on the flipside is also a matter of frequency.

But occasionally someone shows up in our class that neither one of us knows. In this case, the singer songwriter Tom Petty had just passed away. (A founding member of the "Traveling Wilburys") I'm not aware of any connection either I or Jennifer might have had other than being fans of his music. It's only later in this book that I realize my brother Jeffrey had a relationship with Tom; they played softball together at George Harrison's house. I was not aware of that until a year after this following interview.

It's like "six degrees of separation" or as we like to call it *"Six degrees of Kevin Bacon."* I may know someone who knew someone who knows the frequency of someone else. Because I am connected to the person next to me, etherically I have a connection to everyone they've ever met or know. It's also a bit like the admonition of the 80's when people realized when they were "sleeping with a stranger" they were sleeping with everyone that person had slept with. Well, it's kind of like that – but in a positive way.

Everyone you've ever met is connected to you etherically in some way. So ponder that for a moment; everyone you've ever met is connected to each other. And everyone they've ever met is connected to you. Fun thought, isn't it? So if I've met you in this lifetime, I can track you down on the Flipside, and interview you, *even if you won't want to be interviewed. (Scary thought!)*

*****

Jennifer: **Luana is telling the classroom to "be quiet." They're doing an experiment is what I'm getting... Tom Petty is in the back of the classroom.**

Rich: Cool. So how does the class bell work? How do they know when it's "time for class?"

It's a frequency, they know a certain time - it's a frequency that's sent out to everybody...

How many are in the class? Is it whoever shows up with the frequency?

153

There are some people with her, but it goes out to hundreds of thousands that are connected. They don't need to be physically here to be present.

Like a virtual class for the ethernet. Set the classroom visual for me – how is our professor attired?

(Jennifer fans herself) **She is mentioning how hot it is. Hold on – it's interesting to hear they feel the heat...**

How does she look to you?

It's down - she's wearing white – I think I always see her in white. She's changed her lipstick to an orange, like a summer color.

Okay, Luana, what's up? You're here, we're here; let's talk.

She just touched my shoulders. (Jennifer listens) **So I'm getting... She's saying, "Tom Petty wants to know something about his death." I'm saying to her "But he's with you – wouldn't he know about his own death?"**

How can we help him?

He shows me like a computer, googling the answer.

> (Note: I did not "ask for Tom" to come to our class today. This was an example of him passing on, and "showing up spontaneously in the class." In terms of his passing, the results of his autopsy, which showed that he had a massive amount of pain killers in his body from a broken hip, had not been released by this recording.)

What would you like to know, Tom? Can Tom come forward?

"**Yes.**"

I didn't know you Tom, but I likely have friends who knew you.

Luana touches her nose. "**That's why he's here.**"

What would you like to know about your passing?

Does Tom have a daughter?

I think so. Yeah.

It's about someone getting the paperwork. Like whatever help you can give them – they or she - needs to find the paperwork or whatever it was that's necessary for her estate.

But people will handle that, right Tom?

"**Yeah.**"

> (Note: If it's someone we know and they ask "get a message to their loved one;" I'm happy to do so. In this case, I don't know anyone close enough to Tom to say "Hey, your pal asked me to pass this along." That's why I say, "But there are people who will handle that?" - meaning, their *connection* must be better.)

Who greeted you when you crossed over?

His father.

> (Note: I didn't know Tom was physically abused by his father, which led to his heroin addiction. For those who might balk at this answer, as I've reported in "Flipside" people claim that those who abused or

molested them may have asked or been asked to participate in a difficult lifetime to teach or learn the hard lessons that come from that difficult choice. Suffice to say, everyone who knew Tom's dad will reject this concept, but I can only report what people consistently say about the journey; once we "return home" we drop the negative aspects of personality – no matter how cruel or bad – and appear as we exist between lives. People report consistently that "everyone agrees" on what role they're going to play in a future "performance" including the ones who play "the bad guys.")[35]

What was your experience crossing over? Were you startled to cross over?

"Wouldn't you be?"

Were you at home?

He said, "A couple weeks before; his energy was drained," he said he kind of... He said he "felt he knew."

I read an article about you being exhausted. How exhausted were you?

That's what he's saying; he kind of knew. He said, "He told one person that he had a dream about it." It's like he saw it before hand, and told someone about it... he saw a face, from the place where he is now... but it was not the way he dreamt it.

---

[35] https://www.thesun.co.uk/news/4601250/tom-petty-childhood-marriage-breakdown-heroin-addiction/

Did Luana invite you to class to help process this?

"Yes." He looks at Luana. "It (this class) **helps both here and there. It gives it a sort of process... we eventually process everything. An eyewitness.**"

What was your experience crossing over, did you see hear or sense anything?

He's showing me smells... of the concert... whatever is in the concert... smoke...

From pot smoke?

He says, "He quit drinking... 25 years ago."

> (Note: He thought I meant *him* smoking pot, when I meant the usual aroma from a concert. However, this is accurate. In his biography, it's noted he went into rehab for heroin addiction in the late 90's, was saved by his wife Dana.)

What point did you realize you were in the afterlife?

"I saw my dad; he wasn't saying anything, but I could hear his thoughts."

How did he appear? Younger?

The age he last saw him.

Tom, when you look around this group that Luana has assembled, are there other people that you know or a fan of, or surprised to see?

"Yes, really surprised." He's showing me the heart, he was showing me that he knew something was out there (on the flipside) **because of the information he was getting from**

his songs... he was connected back to the place (on the flipside) **where he "downloaded" the songs.**

Beethoven talked about that as well... he credited his music as coming from another universe, or a space beyond time.[36]

I've never heard that.

I have an off the wall question for Luana from someone we know... from a physics professor.

She just rolled her eyes.

If there is an equal amount of matter and anti-matter in the universe, why is there more matter than anti-matter in the universe?[37]

First thing she showed me... she showed me black holes.

Do black holes have anti-matter in them?

"Yes."

So that's why we don't have the same amount of matter and anti-matter in the universe?

She taps her nose (as if to say "correct.")

(Laughs). *If you're correct, then we just won a Nobel prize.*

---

[36] As did Einstein: https://www.nytimes.com/2006/01/31/science/a-genius-finds-inspiration-in-the-music-of-another.html

[37] This is the same question posed by Forbes Magazine: https://www.forbes.com/sites/startswithabang/2018/01/27/ask-ethan-whats-so-anti-about-antimatter/#1b05583c17f0

She was showing me the black hole and the anti-matter inside of it as being more translucent.

This question came up today with physicist Michio Kaku; why there's more matter than anti-matter, because when they meet they explode. But when they measure anti-matter versus matter... it's identical – so they were trying to figure out where the anti-matter is... so your answer is...

"Black holes. **They consume the anti-matter.**"

Kaku said the person who answered this question will get the Nobel.

"**Tell him.** (She pauses) **It's one black hole in particular, not just all of them.**"

One black hole in particular? Is it the one that is considered to be in the center of our universe?

She's showing me one further out.

Where is it? There's reportedly one near the center of the universe.

She showed me light years...

It happened light years ago?

"**But we're now feeling it.**"

So the anti-matter went in one black hole, for the most part?

"**That is correct - to the black holes, but predominantly just one in particular.**"

On the other side of black holes, would we find anti-earth or just matter in some other form?

I got somebody breaking... "physically we'd break apart, going through a black hole." She used Tom Petty for this question.

(Note: I know this doesn't seem like the proper forum to ask questions about physics, but it popped into my mind, so I asked it.)

Tom, welcome to our classroom. So Luana, a mutual friend of ours told me he was driving behind a car and saw something that reminded him of you.

She applauded.

Why?

"In reference to what you're about to say."

Okay. So this friend was driving behind a car and saw that the license plate said "Luana." He emailed me the photo; what was that about?

(Note: He says he's seen this same plate three times.)

"They try to give you information that way. It feels like coincidence, but it's more about energy and synchronicity."

I told this person that I'd talk to you today, and that we are in a "all hands-on deck" situation with regard to saving the planet.

That's why she fanned herself.

(Note: Meaning "global warming" causes the excess heat we're all feeling.)

Well I guess if we lose this planet we won't lose ourselves.

"Right. But it takes a long time to become a civilization again."

> (Note: This is in reference to the idea that we "don't die" even when our planet explodes. We just go somewhere else and begin again – but as she points out, that will take a "long time.")

Why isn't everyone on this side and the flipside trying to stop the destruction of our planet?

"It *is* an "all hands-on deck" situation."

People on the other side are trying to solve it?

"Yes."

Earth is trying to solve it? Humans are trying to solve it?

"Yes."

How can my friend help me get that message onto the planet?

He showed me. (to them) I don't know what that means.

Jennifer specifically or people like Jennifer?

"Intuitives, mediums." But I'm "the front" she said.

The idea of Jennifer leading this research in this fashion? So if I did a book just about our conversations between Jennifer and the class, that's a way to go?

(Luana hits her nose again.)

> (Note: This term "a front" is common in the film business, and was the title of a film made by Woody Allen that Luana and I saw together. I don't know if

Jennifer has ever seen that film, but it's an odd thing for her to say, but not at all odd for Luana to say. She's identifying Jennifer as a "front" for those on the flipside who want to express themselves, the way the "front" in the film was a mouthpiece for blacklisted screenwriters. I would understand this reference, but methinks Jennifer would not.)

Jennifer: I'm seeing that Amelia Earhart tapped you on the shoulder.

(Note: As noted elsewhere, Jennifer and I have had "conversations" with Amelia. I call them that because in all three cases she verified research that I've gathered over 30 years of working on a film about her (I worked on the two films that were made about her) and this research is not in the public domain. There's only one person who could verify these details, and it was her, as reported in "Hacking the Afterlife.")

Rich: Amelia, I know your father was incarcerated for being an alcoholic. Did he physically abuse you?

(She pauses) I'm not getting a *not*. He did when she was younger. It's why she didn't like men. She liked certain men because she knew they'd get her places (she wanted to go)... **but she didn't like them in that way.**

I guess that was part of your journey and path. So how long were you imprisoned in Saipan?

"Seven years."

Did you get to go out around the island ever?

(Jennifer pauses) **"First four years she was able to move around; the last three years she was locked away... but the islanders were trying to help her ... she was well liked by the natives there."**

Was she sick?

"Yeah. Dysentery."

Jumping around a bit. What does Tom Petty think we should call this book?

"Backstage pass." Because we are getting unlimited access to the flipside.

That's what Luana's doing – giving us a "backstage pass?"

I would never ask that question, and she put it in your head... Luana and her friends can also access information you wouldn't think they could.

We can have these "conscious conversations." Like "How do we exist?"

I just saw that the more people know about who we are or were we came from... she showed me a thing going from translucent to matter - the more we understand what's going on, the more fulfilled we are.

And learning this information from them helps us to become more solid or full of understanding?

It comes from (both) **here and there.**

But how does it affect you guys?

She just showed me an earthquake... wait. That scares me a little bit.

Okay, Luana, please give her a different image because she's used to predicting earthquakes... use another metaphor.

(Jennifer smiles) Thank you. **Wow, she showed me a light so intense, it blinded me.** Thank you for that; she's sorry about the earthquake thing. She meant "**It jolts them out of complacency.**" **Whatever we do here, in our class, communicating with them, it helps them, like a loop. Luana just showed me the symbol for infinity.**

A sideways 8. My question is - what would be an example of something we speak about that would help people back there?

She shows me Tom Petty. (Like Tom) **People who just now stepped off the planet... so Tom will be able to believe that he can access friends.**

I would think it would be annoying for someone on that side to wait for months or years to be able to speak to their loved ones, and even after entering their dreams, the loved one says, "I don't believe it was them, I made it up."

My dad has shown up – he says "hello."

Hi Jim.

Thank you. My mom is worried about something to do with my sister and brother, he showed me a whole force of attorneys up there helping them.

So Jim are you telling us attorneys continue to work on the flipside? Just kidding. How do they wind up choosing that occupation in the first place?

164

"It's a frequency – it always comes back to frequency; music arts, movies, literature, the second we get here, we distort it and we forget we have access to it."

So Luana, who is your guide?

"You are."

So when I want to talk to your guide I gotta talk to myself?

She's not kidding.

Luana, during one of my hypnosis sessions, you introduced me to your teacher in your healing class.

Morton just came in... hang on. (It's that) **"You get information from all of them and from the teacher Luana had."**

The story is that in my first session with Jimmy Quast, I went to Luana's healing class, and interrupted them. Then two years later, I did another between life session with hypnotherapist Scott De Tamble, found myself back in her classroom but it felt as if 20 minutes had gone by. During the second session, I became aware she had taken me to meet her teacher after her class, and was saying "This is my friend Richard, he's doing this project back on earth." She was apologizing for me interrupting his class and he looked at me and said, "What do you want to know?" I then asked him questions about what he was teaching, and what the "healing energy of the universe" meant. (Reported in "It's a Wonderful Afterlife.")

Luana had to introduce him softly to you... to have you understand it, because it might have been too abrupt.

I was just thinking about this teacher, and I would say that all the teachers out there – perhaps they're all connected somehow, and it's just the time element is off.

They're all laughing. It's about the time effect you're talking about. My dad just did came forward and said, "I love you Jennifer." Then he told me to "stay away from Prince."

Very funny; a little late now.

(My dad) says "your buddy from the Titanic says, "Thank you." Then he brought in Harry Dean (Stanton). **He said "You made it so much fun at the wake..."**

Harry Dean's memorial? I think people are still talking about it.

They are, trying to figure it out. You sent out a wave they only know; Luana showed me the shock wave that you provided from him. It's so powerful they can't stop thinking about it.

> (Note: As mentioned, I passed Harry Dean's comments along at his memorial service to the individuals he asked me to speak to.)

It's a way of deepening it.

I was writing about a Tibetan meditation, the "Jewel Tree Meditation" where you imagine throwing love and it comes back as a loop.

The infinity figure 8, yeah, the loop. It keeps going, it's going to keep coming back to you over and over again.

Luana just high fived me (for that observation.) Luana just appeared dressed up like a nurse.

That's funny. She played a nurse in our last film together; "The Point of Betrayal" with Rod Taylor.

That was her way of showing me what that means, giving nursing advice to her pals back here.

Jennifer has to run. Tom, welcome, the people in this room can help you in your transitioning.

He says, "They already have."

My problem is, as soon as I mention someone of fame appearing in our sessions, (like Tom Petty) it sounds like I'm selling something. I didn't know Tom, but they're telling you that they did.

They say, "Fuck it."

Does Tom have anything specific he wants me to impart?

He wrote out the word "Spirit." He said "If anyone had any idea how amazing it is to be – not just here, but that's what gives you life here – like having backstage passes. But backstage is... they have it backwards... (The) backstage pass is being alive! That's the pass.

I like that.

Being over here (on the flipside) **is like being backstage but observing everything that is happening – over there on our side.**

So once you're on the flipside, then it's like having a backstage pass?

We get to experience everything immersively. The people outside in the audience; that's the afterlife, those are all the souls watching us perform here on stage. We both have passes; they're just for different dimensions. But the "all access pass" is for all dimensions.

Once you're on the flipside you're observing the stage... back here on the planet?

I would say that people tell us that over here (on the flipside) **we can have "a lot of fun;" you can zip around.**

But they can't feel tactile things or the hard emotions like we do. But they can feel love through us?

"Yes. They feel love through us. Our strongest core, with our heart at peace, is with yourselves. You have to love yourself - that frequency of love is so elevated that they get to feel it; that's the shockwave from them... I think of anger – how anger stops everything... but love allows it (the energy) **to go everywhere."**

Okay, thanks class. See you on the flipside!

*****

Cake for "blu" – the nickname Jack Nicholson gave her

CHAPTER EIGHT:

THANKSGIVING WITH THE COWBOY BUDDHA

Rance Howard in "Ed Wood." Photo provided by Rance.

I met Rance Howard when he came in to audition for my film "Limit Up" in 1998.

The part was to play an older soybean trader from the Chicago Board of Trade. He runs a small firm that has one other trader working for him, Brad Hall, and they employ Nancy Allen as a runner, someone who collects orders from the soybean pit at the Chicago Board of Trade.

The film was based on a true story of a woman I met, who was the only female soybean trader at the Chicago Board of Trade. 500 men refused to trade with her for two years. Day after day she stood in her spot and these men glared at her, stared at her, but refused to take a trade from her.

But then one day they did. And she became the first woman to ever trade in the soybean pit at the Chicago Board of Trade. My brother had a seat in the soybean pit and spent years working his way up. I was fascinated by his journey, but also by the story of this one woman.

Luana and I crafted a story about how this girl works her way up, and then gets an offer she can't refuse. A mysterious woman (Danitra Vance) appears and tells her she can predict how the market will end each day. She claims to work for "Satan" and in return Nancy will have to "sell her soul" to become a successful soybean trader.

Eventually we find out that her boss is Ray Charles, who is actually God. And God appears as a blind sax player who stands in front of the Chicago Board of Trade. (Based on a real blind sax player I saw out in front of the building. I thought "Wouldn't that be funny if depending how much these soybean traders donated, they'd be rewarded by him?")

Most people don't know anything about soybeans or the Chicago Board of Trade. But everything we eat goes through that building and the men who buy and sell these trades are some of the richest on the planet. On busy days it's a madhouse down there, and I wanted to try to recreate something of that insanity.

But the Chicago Board of Trade wouldn't let us in. So we used the Pacific Stock Exchange in Los Angeles and invited 50 soybean traders to come out and be extras in the film. And to our shock, they all agreed. They came out and took over the Beverly Hills Hotel, came to the set in limos, and spent two weeks tearing up Los Angeles.

It's easily the most accurate film about soybean trading ever made. Why isn't it in the public lexicon?

The company releasing it went bankrupt during its release. Also Siskel and Ebert hated the film and gave it a "thumbs way down." As I recounted in "Flipside" Ebert seemed to hate the "spirituality" aspect of the film, didn't believe in the idea of "guardian angels" and both of them trashed the film. Their review effectively ended its run in the theaters, as if I had committed some kind of movie crime.

Perhaps I'll reach out to Siskel and Ebert on the Flipside. (***I do in the final chapter of Book Two! Long after I wrote this sentence! Wow.)*** But this chapter isn't about them or the film. It's about my friend Rance Howard.

Rance was the son of an Oklahoma pig farmer who went to NYC to pursue an acting career. He met his wife Jean on the way, they married and had two famous sons (Ron the film director, and Clint the actor.)

I loved working with Rance. I loved his voice, as it sounded just like my uncle Chuck Knapp, a soybean farmer who I wrote the part in memory of. The film begins with Rance pulling up the Chicago Board of Trade and gives his real wife Jean a kiss on the lips before he heads inside.

Rance's character was based on a story I heard – on a particularly busy day, when the market went "Limit Up" – when traders are frantically trying to get in orders as the price skyrockets - one trader had a heart attack in the middle of those frantic trades. The other traders reportedly stepped over him as the last sounds he heard were the traders screaming "Buy!" "Sell!"

In the film, Rance discovers that Nancy Allen has made a bold move to corner soybeans. He tries to stop her, but has a heart attack while doing so. What Rance and Nancy and Brad don't know in the film – is that Danitra isn't working for Satan. She's working for God, Ray Charles, who has devised this elaborate soybean scheme to get people to give away food for free. There's a little known law "Public Law 480" that dictates when the price of any grain falls below a certain level, they have to give it away to starving countries for free to get the price back up. (*Yawn.* Okay, I get it, who cares about world hunger?)

Anyways, audiences flocked to see "Look Who's Talking" another film made by the same producer Jonathan D. Krane instead of our film – and then the film got lost in a legal custody battle. Last I heard MGM owns it, but can't release it because of a rights issue regarding the music on the film (done by Entertainment Tonight's own John Tesh.)

That's a long way of saying I stayed in touch with Rance. We had lunch on odd holidays *("Hey Rance, it's Arbor day in Canada, should we celebrate?")* Over the next 30 years we had many such lunches or dinners. With Luana, with his first wife Jean, later after Jean died, with his wife Judy, and with my wife Sherry. Lunches and dinners filled with laughter.

At his memorial service, Johnny Depp sent a filmed tribute for him. It was hilarious, with Johnny talking at length about him (they'd appeared in "Ed Wood" and "Lone Ranger" together) and obviously Rance had made an impression on him. **Johnny called Rance "The Cowboy Buddha."**

That's pretty perfect and I wish I'd thought it up. He was a prince among men, never had a bad word for anyone, and saw adversity as it should be seen; something to get through.

I had the good fortune to see him twice before he passed – a long lunch with Brad Hall where we watched a clip from "Limit Up" together on my cell phone. (To which I commented, *"Isn't it funny we made this movie 20 years ago so we could sit here in this restaurant and watch it on my cellphone?"*) .

It was one of Rance's best performances, I felt the most nuanced other than his later work. He was really funny in the part and it reflected the kind a Cowboy Buddha he was.

I offer the following to remind folks who Rance was. But also for them to realize who he still is. **Not gone. Just not here.** But again, I'm not here to offend or upset any of his family, friends or Rance himself. I loved Rance enough to include him as an homage. Even if I didn't believe it was him talking to me (which I do) I'm happy to honor him in some small way. He was and remains *"one of kind."*

*****

Rich: What is today? It's Thanksgiving; we have a lot to give thanks for.

Jennifer: I already have my Christmas tree up.

No way. Is it a real tree?

No, I can't have real trees... it's too painful for me. It sounds weird, but I can hear them dying. I used to get sick every December.

*Okay. That **is** weird. But I love that. So as they're dying you get a sensation in your ear?*

I *hear* them. Trees in general.

That's interesting – it's cutting off the life force I guess. You know, I've talked to people under hypnosis who claim to be able to speak with whatever the life force is in trees. I interviewed a fellow in a redwood forest recently who said the same. He claimed the trees he was talking to directed him to see something that was in the middle of their grove. Something he didn't know – but was there when he found it.

It's kind of like eating meat – but the tree is living in your space, I wouldn't have a cow... (a carcass) hanging up in my house over the holidays.

Ha! Okay, well I agree with you, it's a sentient being that's been murdered on your behalf. But... I think of it as a creature that someone else murdered, and I'm giving it an appropriate sendoff. A celebration.

And you're decorating it.

But I didn't murder it... and the sentient being that is the tree is going back into the flipside, so... it's a good thing.

But I can *hear it dying*! That's important, something that I can't... just can't do it.

So it's a subtle screaming of the tree as it transfers out of here? Wow. Well... but maybe it's a way – I know this sounds weird, but a meditation on the nature of life... If we all go to the Flipside and if all trees go to the Flipside, you are not responsible for murdering the tree. You rescued the tree from the murder zone, and now you can give them an appropriate sendoff... the equivalent of putting up Christmas lights in a hospice... and then if you want, in your mind's eye you can interview the tree.

My dad just interrupted you and said "Interview me! I've almost been gone for a year."

Okay Jim. We will. So class – who's here?

Luana said, "Prince is always late. Robin Williams, he's always first..." My dad said, "He was trying to figure out where it was..." (the class.)

Are they in chairs, or standing up? What comes to mind?

Luana showed me chairs like in a classroom – she went like this (with her hands) **and showed me all the lights, all the thousands of people** (in the wings) **and all the same color.**

So we're like an auditorium? Where the main class is on stage and everyone is outside, like a concert?

There are more people... it's like a football stadium.

Not everyone wants to listen in to our conversation, do they?

Yeah. They do. She showed me... I saw Morty... what's his name?

Michael.

> (Note: Again, for some reason she called Michael Newton "Morton" when he first showed up, and now *he prefers* she call him that.)

He showed me, they showed me that whoever they're connected to... I can see as far back as it goes -- they're

able to bring everyone together, all their souls... all their groups.

Like a giant spider web of connections, or even like Christmas lights on an entire block?

She just showed me the stars. "Yes."

So anyone can listen in if they want. I would guess that all their focus wouldn't be here, because they might be doing something else.

"True. But they can hone in on it..." Luana just showed me Twitter as an example; "The more people that tune in, the more people become aware of it..." it kind of feeds on itself like "headline news" or like "now trending."

That's funny.

She showed me monkeys...

I'd guess that would be a reference to the 100th monkey concept? How one eats a banana differently and then they all monkeys learn that new trick simultaneously?

That's why if one person learns, no one might pay attention, but if 100 people learn, it moves like a wave.

Can anyone ask questions anywhere in the audience?

She just showed me... all these projections of thought. And (how) **she's using her elbows to knock them away.**

She's the matador of this classroom.

She showing me how in my bathroom this morning, I was thinking of my dad, very sad about my dad. Hang on, "sad" is not the right word.

Missing?

In physical form, yes. He's showing me something different. He taught me that's (Jennifer pinches her arm) **the physical form, everything else, nothing can be destroyed...**

But you do get different benefits, your dad can speak to you on a higher level now, that he couldn't do when he was here in a tactile form?

My dad says, "I wouldn't have been able to listen to anyone, including him, especially when I was a teenager. But now I can."

All right Luana, anyone we need to talk to today? The light's on you kid – Your friend Robert Towne said to say hello. I told him I was talking to you. (Her friend the Oscar winning writer/director who gave me my start in the business and appears in Book Two).

She said, "He started this conversation two weeks ago about you, about the flipside, about talking to people on the flipside. He wants to do a movie about it."

Ok. Well probably not with me, but glad he wants to make a film.

I don't know why they are all laughing.

They get it; he wants to do a movie, "just not with me." I pitched something to Universal recently; they said in essence "We love your idea, just not you." That may be why Robert called me yesterday.

She says that Robert doesn't understand it yet. "He doesn't know what to ask."

(Note: I'm remembering another moment in time when Robert was going to have me act in a film after my brief acting appearance in his film "Personal Best." He was writing a film about a mermaid for Warren Beatty, and he created a sidekick named "Martini" and he wanted me to play myself. I was flattered, perhaps flabbergasted, but when they made "Splash" (with Daryl Hannah, whom I had put in her first film, one of my student shorts at USC) my acting career was on *permanent hold*.)

Okay back to class. There's a friend of ours - mine and Luana's - who just crossed over.

She went like this – patting her shoulders. Tuesday. Is that when he passed?

Yes. Is he's still dusting himself off?

Everyone was there, couldn't wait to see him.

Can he come forward? I'll give you his first name; Rance. Rance and I worked together, I saw him twice this past year.

Okay. Hold on. Luana is talking. She says, "She found him." It was like "Could Mr. One million 243 come forward please?"

Right. Pull him out of the audience. He may still be processing.

No, she wants to talk to him. She says he was missing people this year when he was with you... he was talking to you about people he missed.

He knew he was going to die. Even though some people think you (Richard) are crazy, you gave him some amazing insight – he's saying the second time you were together, you gave him amazing advice about the flipside.

> (Note: That is amazingly correct. *(Ding!)* The first time I saw him was with mutual friend Brad Hall, who starred with Rance in "Limit Up." We had some great laughs over lunch, but the second time we met, I took the time to mention this afterlife research. I observed "Most people only find one true love in life. You found two true loves; with your first wife Jean and your second wife Judy, and you had the courage to escort both of them to the other side." A reference to his first wife who he nursed through cancer, and his second who he nursed through Alzheimer's. He said he was "fascinated" by that idea he might have chosen his lifetime.)

He wrote me an email and talked about that.

There's no way you've ever mentioned this to me. (That's correct) **He's so sweet. He says he lost someone... that he lost someone he loved so dearly.**

(Rance's second wife Judy had passed earlier this year. His first wife Jean passed in 2000.)

Was she there to greet him?

He says she was there to "punch him out."

Why punch him out?

"Because it took him so long."

What was it like to cross over?

He's showing me all these sparkles, I feel like he had a dog that came up to him... or somebody that was very close to him... A woman who died of breast cancer?

That was likely his first wife.

She came first and then this other woman came. (Jennifer pauses) Your other buddy is here... Harry.

Harry Dean (Stanton)?

He said, "Thank you." He said, "I can't believe you pulled it off."

You mean talking to your friends at your memorial and letting them know you're "still around?"

He showed me that you talked to his old girlfriend.

*I did. I told Rebecca De Mornay about our conversation with Harry Dean, and she told me she was with him for 12 years. She knew he didn't believe in the afterlife, but when I told her he had a message for her, she screamed **"I knew it!"***

Robin says your work is going to reach the masses; it has to.

Well, you guys have to push it.

They say they're working overtime. I try to tell people "It's not my job to convince anyone there's an afterlife."

It's also important to realize that this inquiry isn't for everyone; not everyone has to know how the play ends.

I don't want to know.

Well, some people feel like I'm showing how the play works or how the novel ends.

Harry Dean just said that; "He didn't want to know it, as it was so painful to think about those friends of his who died."

Yes, he did say that during our interview. Said he "walled himself off from it."

I forgot.

So Rance, you had both your wives come and visit you... what do you think about this adventure - this conversation we're having here?

"Brilliant," he said. Did he speak with an accent?

Yes. A country twang. He was from Oklahoma.

He's such a sweetheart.

He used to sign his emails...

His wife just said "amicably."

Yeah, that's correct. Rance and I worked together on the film "Limit Up" a feature that Luana and I wrote together.

"It had the wrong distribution," he said.

I know.

(Jennifer) But I don't.

Funny, we had lunch with Brad Hall who is married to Julia Louis Dreyfus. They met in college. We watched a clip of "Limit Up" together and I said to Rance "Isn't this funny we made this film together, and now we can watch it in a restaurant on a cell phone? I think we were the only 3 people who saw it."

He keeps saying, "Thank you."

For what?

I don't know. Hold on. **He says, "For helping me understand the afterlife before I was even here."**

So Rance, when we go to your funeral, anything you want me to say to your children?

He's got six... grandchildren.

> (Note: Rance has 4 grandchildren and 2 great grandchildren I'm aware of. *Ding!)*

Show her your sons. One's a film director.

What's his first name?

Ron.

Rance's son is Ron Howard?

Yes, the actor/director. His other son is Clint, also an actor. His granddaughter is Bryce, star of many recent films. They're all really fun people; they got it from Rance and Jean.

He's saying, "His son was very happy you put both his parents in a movie."

Glad to hear it. All right guys, what else?

I'm asking my dad "What did you learn over there over the past year?" He showed me the most beautiful view of the universe.

Who was there to greet your dad when he crossed?

His mom, his dad... He's showing me a lot of people.

I know he was a Mormon bishop. Was he surprised by what he was seeing when he entered the afterlife?

"Yes, it was very spiritual."

Was it related what he expected to see? I thought he might have been surprised with regard to what the Mormon church says about the afterlife. Have I asked him this before?

He said, "No."

If I can ask a religious question. Did Joseph Smith have some kind near death event, vision, or afterlife experience that showed him there was an afterlife? Then when he tried to recreate what he saw, he mixed things up? Like seeing his soul group, came up with that idea we are "sealed in matrimony." That he assumed his soul group was his wives?

"Yes, that's correct. Because we are with our soul group for what feels like forever, because you don't get divorced from your soul group, so it's an experience outside of time."

But I'm asking; was that his soul group that he saw?

"Yes."

When you get married to someone, he assumed that they became part of a soul group by being "sealed"?

"It's more complicated than that."

On the other hand, if you think of all the people helped by Smith's journey, so many Mormons help the poor worldwide, hospitals, etc.

"It wasn't wrong."

But it's like the Jesus story as well. (As we spoke of in "Hacking the Afterlife.") Let me ask; does Jesus ever show up when we're having our classroom conversations?

"He sits somewhere else."

Does that freak people out, students, to see him sitting somewhere in the back of the class, or is that like having a guest celebrity show up?

"They don't look at it like that. He's not there if you don't believe who he is."

Here's what I'm asking; is everybody in the room aware of what I'm talking about?

Wow, ouch. He said, "That's why we can have a class." Hold on a second. **"This class is a different form of communication... it's so much more complicated."** I feel like before... **"it was a different form of communication with people not on the planet, but you're filming it now."**

Let's ask our pal Jesus to come forward, speak to us a bit. I know he's busy, but in this construct, he can be anywhere simultaneously. So asking him to show up is not a big deal.

I selfishly asked him to heal me (of my cold.) **He said, "It will take two weeks."**

That's funny. I had a doctor once say, "If you take a lot of medicine your cold will last two weeks, but if you take nothing it will only last 14 days." Okay, if he's available, I want to talk to him about my uncle who passed a few weeks back.

Was he a priest?

Well... no and yes. Very conservative Catholic. Had 11 hilarious children, seemed like half of Wisconsin was at his funeral. He was very old school conservative, but very funny. During his funeral, I had this vision of him getting the full boat experience, riding on clouds up to heaven...

"It happened. There was a giant beautiful rainbow, and he followed the rainbow up until he got to the end... and when he arrived at the end of the rainbow, it was like this giant gay party going on, and he got upset."

That's funny.

Because he was looking around, "Where am I?" and all these guys and girls making out. He was like "Oh no, I'm in the wrong rainbow!"

That's hilarious.

I just got shown the car that Harry Dean and Luana were in, on their way to that music fest... And how when they had a flat tire, it was at that moment that Harry Dean realized he was in the afterlife, since the flat tire wasn't part of his memory. That's when your uncle realized the afterlife wasn't what he thought it would be.

Like "This ain't heaven. I must be in the other place!"

It was too much for him.

Luana, you met my uncle. Can you access him? Or is he busy doing penance in limbo?

He's there. He's laughing his ass off.

> (Note: My cousins from Milwaukee are flat out the funniest people I've met. I've been to way too many funerals with them, and come away from the experience saying, "I've never laughed so hard in my life." That's a testament to their mom and dad; both raised a bevy of kids who appreciate laughter, tenderness and a kind word.)

The biggest thing is... (They're saying) "We wasted so much time thinking..." They're laughing, **"We wasted so much time thinking about what's right, what's wrong – we wasted so much time. If we had just been open we would have experienced so much more."** They're showing me just soaring.

Who's the predominant speaker of this thought?

Luana is like "Who do you think?" She's doing the filtering.

A profound thing to speak about. "Don't waste your time worrying about what's right or wrong."

"Stop thinking about how to live. Stop thinking about how to live and just live." Or like Nike; "Just do it."

Funny. "Nike" was a character in the film Luana and I co-wrote, "Limit Up" – it starred Rance Howard and Danitra Vance, who is also on the flipside.

I was shown Lenny Kravitz's daughter. Robin wants to say something.

Yes, Danitra did look like like Lenny's daughter; African American with wild hair. I interrupted Robin, what did he want to say? Who are you making laugh over there?

"Me," he says. He wants to say to **"Never give up."** He's concerned **you** get frustrated.

Does he mean give up this flipside work or the movie work?

"Give up on the movie work. It will come to you."

Okay. "Easy for you to say."

"Let it go. Just focus on this work and all the other stuff will come in. You try to focus on something else and it cuts you off from everything."

That's funny advice. "Hey Rich, that movie thing you've been doing for 30 years? Give it up dude." What about Amelia? You want me to let your film project go as well?

She shakes her head "No. Don't let it go. Just don't focus on it; it will come to you. Make it about the work. Take a step back."

It's funny how you and I talked about her being arrested and dying on Saipan (in "Hacking the Afterlife") Another guy came out the other day in USA Today saying the same thing.[38]

I described Saipan for you and I'd never heard of the place.

---

[38] https://www.guampdn.com/story/news/2017/11/25/chamorro-man-supports-theory-earhart-held-prisoner-saipan/883664001/

True, Jennifer, you even drew a precise map!

> (Note: The first time I met Jennifer, I asked her to clarify what she was "seeing" and she drew a map of Saipan, roads I had just been, including a church, a parking lot, and a precise location of where I had been.)

*Amelia, it's not about me finding you, is it? It's about the **world finding out who you really were**.*

She says "Way too much time has been spent searching for her. It's not about finding her, its about finding everyone else in the ethers through her, through this process."

I guess proving what happened to her (and her plane) would be a powerful statement of our ability to "speak to the dead."

"To the "alive." **Backstage pass** is the best title for our new book; "Stop thinking!"

What does that mean?

"Stop thinking about what's right or wrong; just stop thinking! Just live." It's funny how much they want to rush this book into print.

It's important to repeat our conversation with Harry Dean which proves he was talking to us, beyond a shadow of a doubt.

He says, (referring to Jennifer) "that *I am* cute."

The idea I could use my friendship with Harry as verification and my relationship with Luana and you to verify it...

Luana says "The verifiable information is going to do more."

Oh, tell Rance I'm taking my family to his memorial.

He says "Yeehaw!"

Catch y'all next week. Class! Be on time!

*****

The Howards; Ron, Rance, Clint & Jean

CHAPTER NINE:

ROBIN THE GENIE

"Irony"

Another session with Jennifer at a restaurant in Manhattan Beach. (Thank you *Fishbar* for letting me film Jennifer in a booth in the back. "A wonderful place to talk to spirits and enjoy great seafood!) This chapter was originally a little bit later in this book, but it had to be moved. You'll understand why, somewhere in the midst of this chapter.

Robin Williams (or what appears to be Robin) makes an appearance in *"Hacking the Afterlife."* We asked him if he would give me a quote to put on the jacket of the book, and he said, **"Love love."** As in "Love what love is." At some point, I was trying to cut down the size of "Hacking" and cut out his chapter. Imagine my chagrin when the following week, Jennifer said "Robin is here and he wants you to put it back." "What?" I asked. "Something about him in the book."

*How do you **not** listen to what people are telling you from the Flipside?*

I make no claim that this is Robin speaking to us from the great beyond. But I do have many friends who knew him well, and as reported, I had the pleasure of dining with him. I consider him an avatar of healing – as people who perform the kind of life changing comedy that he did are like shamans or surgeons. People feel better merely seeing one of his films, or laughing at his wit – he's healed millions of souls. For that alone, he deserves to be highlighted here.

*****

Rich: I was just transcribing a session we did – April two years ago! We were talking about "Akashic libraries," and we talked about what it looked like for you to pull a book out of the stacks of "lifetime histories." You described the book as "clear energy" – yet it was someone's lifetime. Very in depth and unusual. Luana makes an appearance in that session; we didn't have a class then.

Jennifer: **We did, but we didn't know it.**

Ok. Who's here?

Luana. The guy who looks like Cronkite; Morton. "Morton Cronkite."

Michael Newton? I think he looks more like Chuck Heston. Michael, it's a bit unusual for you to be front and center here, what do you want to tell us?

He wants you to know – he's giving me a picture of you in my mind – he **wants you to "Not to become frustrated with the details. Of what it is you're writing about." He says**

"He's doing more work over here... He's talking about having efficiency in talking or conversing about spirit."

He's saying I should be more efficient when helping people to talk to spirit or that I should be more efficient?

He says that you block it.

Are you talking about when I'm trying to write a chapter?

He's showing you outside on your back porch... on your balcony... in your rock garden... amid your pet rocks.

Rocks I've picked up around the world... some are from my trek to Tibet; should I somehow focus on them?

"No," he says, "There's a part of you that gets so much happening on the computer and you become hyper-focused and it pushes away what comes in."

He's talking about automatic writing? Just to set the table so to speak, take a pen and paper and say, "What's up?"

Jennifer taps her nose.

> (Note: That's how I wrote Luana's version of the foreword to this book.)

Pay attention, focus and unfocus?

"Allow."

Should I be...

I just asked that question – "Should you be asking questions to get an answer?" **No, just start off with "What's up?" A lot of times they give you the question to ask.** But they're showing me even when they give you the question to ask, you'll switch it.

I can type pretty fast; as fast as I can talk. Okay, Michael that's a good tip; very interesting.

Your mom says "Sorry... about the scar on your face!"

> (Note: I was sleeping with our cat on my chest, and awoke to have the cat clawing my face and jumping off. Took a pretty big slice of my chin. When I mentioned it to Jennifer, she correctly identified where I was in the house, how I was asleep, and said our cat saw the "etheric presence of my mother walking" in the room. Meow!)

Jennifer: **Your mom says your son had a question about a certain section of music – a piece of what he was playing and he was stuck on, performing, and she came to help him – and scared the cat, and the cat landed on your face.**

> (Note: Mom was a concert pianist, our son just magically picked up the piano, plays complex pieces without any sheet music.)

Rich: It's amazing – he listens to the music in a film and sits down to play it.

She just blew on her knuckles... (a gesture of pride).

Good job Anthy. I assumed someone threw the cat at me as a joke.

Your cat opened her eyes... saw your mother walking through/behind your chair to get to your son, she showed me where your son was sleeping next to you.

Very interesting. Who else?

My dad.

Jim! Happy anniversary.

Yeah, how's your first birthday over there? He says, "It's not all it's cracked up to be – he showed me a little toy "whoo hoo!" He's showing me the full moon from the (recent) eclipse, he said he put a bubble around me when I went swimming with the sharks in Tahiti. I had a calmness during that, the same calm when I jumped out of the plane to skydive... Remember how I said they help focus the awareness? Which reminds me of a client who was in the shooting in Las Vegas. And she came in and wanted to know if her dad had helped her survive that shooting.

Wow.

She was in Vegas during the shooting, she went under the stage... and described this calmness that came over her... this peacefulness. What I was getting from her spirit was that her dad helped her focus on her hands – She said she didn't see any of the mayhem, she didn't see people being shot or dying, and she knew that was him because of the awareness.

Like a protective bubble?

It was the same thing for me when I jumped out of a plane to skydive. I remember my awareness was on my hands when I jumped. Her dad was able to help her focus on her hands to calm her heart down, so she wouldn't see the bloodshed. Her boyfriend was counting the rounds, when he said the shooter was done – they bolted. But he wasn't done, the shooting started again, but they still ran and got out of there.

We talked to Jim recently, asking him about being able to visit the moon in spirit form.

They were all laughing about that.

He said it was difficult to go to places he hadn't been – but it's easier to go to a place if your frequency has been there – then we talked about going to Mars.

They're showing me Elon Musk.

What does David Bowie think of this homage to him? Playing "Major Tom" on a Tesla for a billion years?

Who's doing that?

Elon.

I was shown Elon Musk right before. I haven't heard about this.

Elon Musk sent a Tesla into outer space playing David Bowie's song "Ground Control to Major Tom." It's a red Tesla convertible with a fake astronaut in it, and he's already broadcast photos of it going around the earth... It's on its way around the sun and go into orbit on Mars – for a billion years. Talk about setting a high bar for a memorial! So David Bowie will be singing over Mars the next billion years. What does Mr. Bowie think about that?

He's there... hang on a second. (Listens) **David says, "He thinks it was a waste of money."**

Okay.

He's so sweet - he says he wishes the money was used differently... says the environment could do more with the money.

We can.

Wait, I got a glimpse of something – intriguing – I asked him, "Can't you just send someone here from the future to figure out how we can help the environment?"

If we suddenly saw someone from the future, it would screw up everyone's path here on the planet.

He's showing me green lights... It felt like it was coming from the essence of other souls that are doers... that help do whatever you're talking about.

I was just wondering if you could play with the Tesla toy sent in your direction from where you are on the flipside.

They showed me that up there, people are in line waiting to see that on the other side. Like waiting to see the Statue of Liberty.

David, you obviously moved or influenced Elon Musk's life.

Hold on – he doesn't mean to say that he doesn't have gratitude for it; he says "It's a cool thing. The world needs more people like Elon." And he just showed me Richard Branson.

People who think about side the box?

That don't have limitations.

Jennifer, did you see the Super Bowl performance in Minneapolis and the tribute to Prince?

No. I was on a plane.

Prince, can you show Jennifer what Justin Timberlake did at the Super Bowl, if you care to?

Gosh. He showed me like being immersed in Justin Timberlake's body, like completely connected. And then looked behind him... There was something behind him, a big screen; I'm being shown a giant screen.

That's right. They had a big screen of Prince dancing behind Justin. On Jimmy Fallon, Justin said he was shocked how the images were in synch with the original soundtrack, and he said he thought Prince had done that himself.[39]

Prince says he manipulated the editor. Said it was easy "because he was stoned."

That's funny. (Who knows? No way of verifying that one. Apologies if you weren't; edit team.) Justin said they used the original stems from the song, and then when they put it to the footage that they have of him from Purple Rain it matched – magically. So what did you think about that Mr. Nelson?

Prince said, "It was great to be out there again." He's showing me looking at the stage, looking at everyone in the crowd. He's showing me how happy he was when Justin

---

[39] From Variety "Timberlake (paid) tribute to Prince during his set, ...with 90's-era images of the singer projected onto a billowing screen above the stage, evoking both Prince's classic era and his own galvanizing Super Bowl Halftime performance in 2007." http://variety.com/2018/music/news/super-bowl-halftime-producer-talks-justin-timberlake-prince-and-confirms-never-a-hologram-1202690054/

performed; that it "came from God." He didn't sing Purple Rain, did he? I'm hearing he did not.

It was "I Would Die 4 U." Anything else Mr. Nelson?

Huh. He says, "He wants to be chapter nine."

Why?

I don't know.

Chapter Nine. Okay. I think I've figured out how to tell our story... using these clips as a series of interviews.

Morton (Michael Newton) showed up. He says, "I told him he'd figure out a way to tell the story more efficiently." Morton says he will help you with the format.

Very good, okay class. Who else?

My dad is showing me that the energy of the planet isn't grounded.

Jim, you're feeling the energy is different for you since we started doing this work – or different altogether?

"Recently."

What do you attribute that to?

He's showing me that the planet is going through a different phase of energy, if you're more open to it – he showed my feet being off the ground.

Let's bring forth a scientist to ask why the earth feels not grounded. Is Julian Baird available?

I just saw what's his name... Carl Jung.

You saw Carl Jung or a photo of him?

Photo. **Julian had something wrong with his heart? He looks pasty or pale. He's showing me ...**

He had leukemia. Is he the right person to ask about this grounding of the planet?

He just went like this - "squinting his eyes" at you. (Note: Funny, it's a face he used to make. I'm questioning if he's the right "scientist" to be asked.) **And then showed me it's like we're being pushed and pulled. It's like we're going so fast, it's hard for things to catch up - that's why someone like me doesn't feel grounded.**

We've heard people talk about the ley lines of the planet, the grid being adjusted.

"Yes."

I've heard some claim they work on adjusting the protective grid around the planet to help open up consciousness. Is it related to that?

"Yes." Okay I'll try to describe this – I got shown the earth wrapped up in a bubble, when everything is dense... And now things are beginning to open up and everything starts floating up – everything is connected, but it's no longer dense. When everything is separate, it lifts... it gets opened up, so people don't know what the difference is any more.

So that connectedness is disconcerting people?

"Yes, that's why some people are leaving the planet."
Robin Williams is saying – because he left the planet –
subconsciously... they're reminding me...

Let's address that. Robin, your decision to leave the planet was based on the fear of losing your conscious mind?

"Irony," he says.

One truth is that you could have stuck around, gone through that experience of losing your mental ability and you still would have wound up in the place you are, correct?

"Yes." He's spelling it out for me; "I R O N Y."

But in terms of people feeling less grounded...

Let's ask; "are we supposed to be more grounded or more connected?"

Okay, let's ask that – who wants to take that?

Robin is saying, "Yes. But not in the way that you think. We should be grounded. But instead of being grounded to our lower half, our lower chakras, we need to be grounded to our upper chakras, connected to our source, (that) is the way to be."

I understand.

I don't. I've never been shown this before. **If you're centered "this way"** (from above to below) **everything else is fine.**

I take it to mean that if you're connected to your higher consciousness, the two thirds of our conscious energy that we always leave behind, we'll feel more centered. So it doesn't matter what's going on with the earth – as long as you're connected spiritually, that is our center?

They're showing me that when I'm connected that way (to spirit) **I feel grounded.**

It's counter intuitive then; reverse grounding?

"Irony!" says Robin.

If you're here below, you're in the mesh, in the throes of gravitational pull, or polarized by positive and negative. But if you're focus is back there – back home - you're observing things here but are not controlled by them?

"The whole planet is changing, there are more shark attacks than before, nature is reacting to the water being polluted, global warming is changing that."

Okay, Julian, so how do we fix that? I'm talking about the next 50 or 100 years, is there anything we can do actively in the next 100 years that we can pass along to humans to say simply; start doing this.

"Save water."

What about changing salt water to fresh water; will that help?

They showed me Elon Musk again – I wonder if he's working on that? He's more receptive.

Everyone? How do we change salt water to fresh water for pennies?

Huh. They just showed me mud – as a filter ... as the water goes through the mud, it rises, evaporates... if we get water

and put it through mud – then I saw it gets dried up and the top being taken off. The salt goes.

Filtering it through mud? How do we speed that up or do that? It is kind of how it works – salt water rises into the clouds, and fresh water comes down – without the salt.

They showed me a mesh. Harness it, they say.

Who would be able to do that?

"Einstein."

Let me ask you guys this: in terms of us helping us alter the course of the planet, I'm assuming someone will read what we're talking about and it will influence them in a positive way.

"Yes." He also showed me a monk – a Buddhist monk – I saw lights and a monk.

You're saying monks can meditate on these things and get the answers as well?

"Yes."

We can't solve these issues but we can help lead the people to the solutions.

They said, "They're way ahead of you on that."

Very difficult to manipulate events here.

"In the way you're thinking, yes."

How are you guys thinking?

They put our awareness towards certain things... We just need to be open to them. When I was talking to that girl who survived the shooting at Vegas with the help of her father who had died, I asked her dad, "How did you get them out of there?" He said, "I made them really want to go to the bathroom so bad, they would leave" and my client later said, "My boyfriend had to go to the bathroom so badly, he had to run out of there."

The father gave me evidence of all the things he put their awareness towards; being incredibly hungry, etc, to get them out of harms way. It didn't alter the event, no, but their outcomes might have been different. I asked them "Did you know what the outcomes would be?" They didn't know the outcomes for each person...

Another question would be, in terms of chaos vs. order, in that shooting event in Vegas, there were a certain amount of people who were trying to escape, but others who had agreed to cross over, by prior agreement. Is that correct?

"Yes." He showed me – Her father was a retired cop – he had several people who helped him wrap a bubble around them so they could leave.

But it's not like he was there to protect them from this event?

"No."

But to assist them from what he knew was supposed to happen?

"Yes."

Okay. Anyone else in class?

Hold on. Robin Williams is literally screaming "Good morning... what is that?"

"Good Morning Vietnam?" Let's ask him. Why are you screaming, dude?

He's shouting "LIFE! That we're all learning!"

Are people surprised when they see you on the flipside, Robin?

They don't believe it.

Who's more popular? You or Jesus?

I *am* Jesus! (He laughs.)

Okay, Jennifer has to get back to work. See you all on the flipside.

*****

With Mark Damon in "The Young Racers." Francis Coppola was the sound man; asked Luana to be in "Dementia 13."

CHAPTER TEN:
BILL FROM TEXAS
"It's fun. I can fly"

Bill Paxton and his father John. Photo: Wikimedia

We've mentioned Bill a number of times in various chapters. But I went back and put together a loose collection of the times that he showed up when I was speaking to him (or with another medium later in this chapter.)

After Bill started showing up, I've reached out to his family and friends. He had specific messages for me to pass along to them, and I did so via mutual friends. In these two following interviews with Bill, I deliberately didn't tell Jennifer or medium Kimberly Babcock who he was. **Not because I have any doubts about this process, but because I didn't want his fame to get in the way of our conversing.**

As noted, I've known Bill since the beginning of his career. We met in London while he was on the set of *"Aliens"* and we were going to make my film *"You Can't Hurry Love"* together." (He helped me rewrite the script.) We hung out a bit, and spent a few fun evenings together in Cannes over the years.

Last time we spoke on the phone was to invite him to a screening of my film *"Cannes Man"* in Santa Monica. I did not see him at the screening but heard his distinct laughter. That same laugh that I heard in a pub in London which I recognized immediately as the "crazy brother" from the John Hughes film *"Weird Science."*

Again, apologies in advance; not trying to upset or offend any of his family, friends or fans with this conversation with Billy on the flipside, but as you'll hear in this chapter, he does quite a bit of verification for us on many levels.

*****

Rich: We have a mutual friend who passed away recently, Luana, his name is Bill.

Jennifer: They just danced.

Who just danced?

Bill and Luana did a little tango thing.

> (Note: Bill met Luana before his career took off, he was going to star in my film *"You Can't Hurry Love"* which Luana appeared in as well. Luana was always a big fan of Bill and his work, so it's not unusual to hear they met up on the Flipside.)

Does Bill want to talk to us?

He just showed me him filing his nails... (Like *"Yeah, what is it?"* Bill and my relationship was always in the poking fun at each other in this realm.)

He's here?

He says, "He's shampooing his hair, getting ready."

Tell us what it's like over there.

"It's fun," he says. He says, "I can fly" and that he likes scaring people.

Who was the first person to greet you when you crossed over?

"His dad."

> (Note: Bill's father did precede him in death, and as we'll hear from another medium, he says the same thing to her.)

Was that a happy reunion?

He says it was "Shocking because that meant that he had died." He said "Yes, at first, it was shocking, but then that subsided." At first, he was startled. **"It wasn't scary," he says. "It was like a recognition of both worlds." He showed me them together.**

Was this an "exit point" for you? Something that you planned to have happen? Was this the right or wrong time for your exit?

> (Note: "Exit points" are something we've learned in these interviews. People say that we generally stay here to accomplish what we've set out to do, but "exit ramps" or "exit points" sometimes appear, and we wind up leaving earlier than we thought we would.)

He's saying, "It was the wrong time for his physical body, it was the right time for his soul."

You once talked about going to visit the Titanic. What was that like?

(Jennifer stops, makes a face, eyes wide.) Is this the Billy that was in the movie "Titanic?" He showed me a picture of that guy who just passed. I'm so confused.

Well, let's ask him. Is that picture that Jennifer is seeing of a person, is that a picture of you? If it isn't, give her a thumbs down.

He gave me a thumbs up. This is him? I saw him here, in the office when we met the other day... I love Billy, I had no idea...

He and I met in London when he was making the film "Aliens," my old high school friend Lori was friends with his then girlfriend, later wife Louise. We all went out for a pint, and when he laughed uproariously, I recognized the laugh from "Weird Science." We had John Hughes in common, John went to my high school. Later I asked Bill to star in my first film "You Can't Hurry Love," it didn't happen, but I used a song from his band Martini Ranch (no relation) to open the film. I hadn't seen him in years before he passed. Bill, take Jennifer down with you in that capsule when you went to see the Titanic.

> (Note: Bill had worked with Jim Cameron before and when Jim took him to see the Titanic, Bill initially thought he would see it from a camera on the ship's deck. But Jim put him in his bathysphere and together they made a number of trips to see the Titanic.)[40]

(Staring into the distance, Jennifer shivers.) **I got scared because of the water rushing** (past) **but then he grabbed my hand and he calmed my heart down.** (Jennifer pauses) **He's taking me to a corner, he's showing me the boat. If you had a blueprint of the boat we're going to the farthest right corner of the Titanic... okay...** (To Bill) **Go slower. He just told me, "You don't have to hold your breath."**

Describe what you're seeing and feeling.

I'm feeling a sense of peace. I'd be really scared to ever go into something like that. He's taking me down to the right of the bow... that's below on the bottom, in the front, and there's a hole in the front – he showed me an explosion... an explosion that caused that hole. It's in the front.

> (Note: *Ding!* This is accurate. Jim Cameron has taken 33 trips to visit the Titanic. National Geographic did an extensive survey of the wreck, and it does include a hole where she's describing it. Knowing Jennifer as well as I do I'm confident she's not referring to

---

[40] Oddly enough, in April 2017, a few weeks after this interview, a "locket" from the Titanic was found on the ocean floor in a bag.

something that she's seen, but something that she is "seeing.")

They hit the iceberg on the right side.[41]

I didn't know that.

Okay, thanks Billy. Let's move on to some other questions.

It's funny; I feel like I'm decompressing now.

Bill, have you seen John Hughes since you got back?

(Jennifer laughs) He says, "He's really busy."

Anything you want to say to Jim Cameron?

"Thank you." He said it again, "Thank you."

Anything more specific?

He said, "He knows where it is."

Where what is?

Something they were looking for? Jewelry?

I don't know. I thought that was made up. Where is it Billy? Is he showing you a jewel?

He's saying to be quiet. He showed me you interrupting him... he says, "I'm trying to talk."

Sorry.

He's saying it's something that was lost on the ship. (Oddly enough, a few weeks after this, they found more artifacts near

---

[41] http://www.dailymail.co.uk/news/article-2118217/New-Titanic-images-doomed-ship-youve-seen-before.html

the ship, including jewelry) **He's showing me a future project with Jim... Might be a movie, something they talked about.**

Is that something you were going to be involved with?

He's showing me looking at papers, but I don't know.

Well, I can't really call up Jim and ask him, but Billy, you know how to whisper in his ear.

"I know how to scare him," he said.

That's allowed. Let's talk about other stuff. What do we look like to you? How do you communicate with us?

(Jennifer laughs.) **He says so many funny things. He just showed me an image of my** (backless) **dress and said, "I can almost feel it." I'm asking, "Are you kidding around, or just being Bill?" He said, "I'm being Bill." He showed me the aerial view of being above us, your head, he says he sees eyes because they're windows...**

Windows of the soul?

That works best, the eyes, that's what he sees.

Can you physical manifest something over here? Like move a napkin, or make a splash in water?

He says, "You'd have to be Einstein."

> (Note: This is a reference to the math involved. What people consistently say is that in order to create an image over there, it's a math equation that they work on and learn how to do. In order to create a message or a sensation or an image for someone over here, it's

also a math equation. They can get a person to "see something" that they didn't notice before, but generating the message (via math) to their mind, to get them to notice the object. But he's saying, in order to "manifest" over here, which includes appearances, etc, it would require "higher math.")

Are you familiar with film director Tony Scott?

Bill says he is. Seems like he met him.

What happened with Tony Scott?

Bill made an X with his hands. I don't know why.

Are you referring to "X box drug" he was taking when he jumped off a bridge? Or are you just saying X?"

Just X.

Bill can you pull Tony in?

"Yeah." Did he have light eyes?

I don't know.

(Note: They're Hazel)

He looks English.

He was. We have friends who asked about you. What was the cause of you checking yourself out? Robert Towne asked me about it.

He says, "He thought he could fly."

Very funny. (I'm being sarcastic. I realize Jennifer doesn't know who he is, but Tony pulled over on the Vincent Thomas Bridge in San Pedro and jumped to his death).

He just showed me the film "Birdman." The film with Michael Keaton.

About a man who learns he can fly. Okay. But at some point, you are driving over the Vincent Thomas bridge and you pulled over and jumped. Was that related to your path and journey, or was it and adverse reaction to drugs in your system?

He says "both." He says it actually prevented him from hurting other people. The way he's showing me... He says "I would have hurt more people. I had my out, it was my time, that was my out."

Did the medicine – the black box drug you were taking for insomnia have anything to do with it?

He showed me he was mixing everything.

Anything to say to your brother Ridley?

"Tell him it doesn't run in the family."

Anything to demonstrate to your brother this is you?

"Remind him that he still has my chair."

What about Robert Towne?

Tell him "I'm sorry." There was something unfinished about them, a project they were working on. He says he's sorry that he didn't finish the work with him.

What's it like over there for you, Mr. Scott?

He flies. He showed me flying. He's joking, but that's literally what he's doing. Hang on. Was Bill Paxton like this in life? He keeps interrupting me, he said "You called him Mr. Scott but you didn't call me Mr. Paxton!"

Tony is showing me looking over the ocean. I'm asking him, "What are you doing?" And he said, "I'm researching where I'm supposed to have my next life."

That makes sense. Get a preview of where you might go next?

I'm asking, "Are you researching your next life sequentially?" He showed me the past... I asked, "If you go back in time do you screw up the future?" He showed me all the acts of a play, each lifetime is like an act of a play, you can go back in and revisit that act, re-experience it.

Do you mean. not that you're trying to alter the play, but you can go back and re-experience that play, that second act, so you can learn more lessons from that experience?

He said that's how Deja vu is created.

So in this vast sea of experience, you can revisit any experience that occurred so that you can gain insight from it?

They just showed me how your mind works, they're fascinated how you take in this information...

My mind? Oy. But it's important to point out that we're altering our own future by going back in time to reexamine the past. But doing so, we actually change the past because we see it for what it was, lessons and learning. By doing so we also can change our spiritual future, because we've re-examined why things happened. Is that correct?

"Yes."

Bill, you also said your experience over there was that you were learning how to fly. Can you show Jennifer how you can fly from one place to the next?

He's showing me (visually) **before I can really process it. He's going to all these corners really fast, then he showed me how many things are going on in the interim. Then he slowed it down, super slow and showed me how things move here - but he's going faster than that.**

You mean like a super fast game of Pong or tag? And he slowed it down so you only see four or five touches?

"Yes."

> (Note: I once heard "EVR" voices on video that could only come from someone on the flipside. I sped up the speed of their voices one and a half times until they sounded "normal." I've heard often that "hearing" or "seeing" people on the flipside is a frequency adjustment. It's not clear if slowing down or speeding up their frequency would be effective; as we'll learn "both sides" need to make an adjustment.)

Describe what do we look like to you; how do you communicate to us?

He showed me the aerial view from above us, he showed me your head. He said, "What works best is the eyes, as they're the windows to the soul."

If you were going to pick some aspects of life on the planet that you might miss, or wish you could live again?

He showed me a pistol, chewing tobacco, horses...

He misses chewing tobacco?

No, he's showing me like another lifetime.

Where was that?

In Texas. Near Austin. Feels like after the civil war... after 1879.

> (Note: Bill goes on to describe in detail a former lifetime, details of which I was able to verify through research. It involved a small group of Mormon settlers who lived near Austin, and he was showing her a lifetime where he was the leader of that group.)

Bill any of your old girlfriends I need to reach out to tell them you said hello?

"I had no old girlfriends. I only had eyes for my wife."

That was just a test buddy.

He's laughing.

What can we ask you that an average person might ask? What's your day like? Do you sleep?

"There's no sleeping there."

Do you have a place that you like to hang out?

He's showing me on a white beach.

For relaxation?

"Yeah. To think."

What do you think about?

"How he wants his next life to be."

Tell us, what will it be? Any idea?

He says he wants the world to be a better place.

How can you help effect that?

He showed me someone like Elon Musk, someone who knows how to get things done or made.

So how do you create your white beach? How do you create objects over there?

He said, "It's by using mathematics and science." He says, "He puts an equation together that gets him the right (visual or) **taste of whatever you want to drink or experience. Whatever you're looking for.**"

So when you want to experience a white beach it's a mathematical equation?

"It is, but you don't have to take it to that extent. It just happens."

Let me ask you about other realms. I know that Jim Cameron said he had a vision of Navoo, the planet or people that are in Avatar. What was that about?

He's laughing. Says, "They *were* Martians."

I mean was his dream in high school related to seeing something that actually exists somewhere else, or was it created by his mind? Or do you know?

He said, "Be patient." He's trying to show me. He showed me Africa. Did Jim Cameron's father go to Africa? There's something with an African influence for Jim Cameron – he showed me a mask, something with a mask, obviously we don't see that in the movie, but it was the same recurring dream over and over again, it's about helping the planet. He wanted to help the planet.

I know Jim had a dream about the Terminator while sitting in a pensione in Italy; he dreamed about the skeletal Terminator robot.

"He gets those dreams about the future..." I just got shown our friend Scott De Tamble.[42] Sometimes under hypnosis people can access the future.

But I'm asking does the planet from Avatar exist somewhere?

"Yes."

In our universe or in another realm?

Bill is so funny. If I'm interpreting this correctly, he's saying, "It does exist somewhere else, and when you're able to link in, you can get the information from there to manifest itself here. But more importantly, nature, the trees that exist on our planet have existed longer than any humans. And what happens in the film, is happening here on our planet. For example, when we take down trees in the Amazon or in Africa we are cutting off the life support in other dimensions."

---

[42] Scott's a hypnotherapist trained by Michael Newton: lightbetweenlives.com

I don't understand that, but okay. Billy, is there anything you want me to pass along to your family and friends?

"**Reach out to them,**" he says.

I know his children are on social media, but I don't want to be like a creepy uncle. I mean, who wants to hear from some dude who claims he's talking to your loved one?

"**Get over it,**" he says.

Give me something to say that your friends and family would know comes from you.

"**When one of them has a dream about him, that's him trying to get through. There are changes, or decisions being made, and he wants them to know whenever they ask him questions, he's there trying to help out.**"

So your message is; "Listen?"

"**Bingo.**"

Should I tell them the Michael Newton method (that Jennifer and I heard in another interview with the Flipside) "Say the name of your loved one, either aloud or in your mind, ask them questions you don't know the answer to, when you hear the answer before you can form the question you'll know you've made a connection?"

"**Yes, but without mentioning Michael Newton.** (Jennifer laughs) **Whatever it takes; it's important.**" He showed me that Jim Cameron is thinking about doing a project about the afterlife. So if you talk to him, ask him about it.

I will. Thanks Billy.

*****

So that was a transcript of the film I shot in Jennifer's office, when Bill first made an appearance. Then a few days later, I got a call from Dr. Elisa Medhus, who was asking me to meet some mediums who were going to start working with her and her son Erik. (As noted elsewhere, her son speaks to her from the flipside via different mediums. Excerpts of some of this conversations appear in earlier books.)

In this case, she asked if I would meet Kimberly Babcock, a medium who also happened to be a minister. She was in town for some meetings and I took the opportunity to interview her. Over the course of a couple of hours, we talked about her journey to spirituality, but towards the end of the interview, I thought "Oh, here's a chance to interview another medium about what Bill might have to say from the Flipside."

He met at Hugo's restaurant in West Hollywood. They were reluctant to let me use my camera during the interview, so I had to use shorthand in some cases. But the following is a transcript of that footage. After a discussion of her journey into mediumship, I said:

Rich: Can you bring my friend Bill forward?

Kimberly: "Bill has been waiting for you."

Hi Bill. What do you want to say to your family or friends?

Was he not able to say goodbye before he passed?

That's correct.

He's showing me it must have been quick or there was no closure when he passed.

Well, this is a way of helping give closure; what would you like to say?

That's it; "That I have closure and that "I'm at peace." He says, "He knows he didn't get to say goodbye, that they still have that wound, because there was no closure before he passed because he didn't get to say goodbye before he passed."

What does he look like to you?

I don't see him at all. I just sense him. **Did he have issues with his chest? I'm feeling like his passing was very quick. He said, "I'm sorry."**

To who?

"To them." Was he on medication or something with medicine?

He was getting an operation, they were working on his heart.

I think it's more than that; medicine was involved with his health and his passing. He's showing me a pill bottle, as if they were giving him medicine.[43]

Okay. So now you're back home – are you there with your soul group? Who greeted you when you crossed over?

His dad. I see the word "dad" written in the air.

> (Note: Same answer to my earlier question to Jennifer Shaffer.)

---

[43] https://www.mirror.co.uk/3am/celebrity-news/weeks-before-bill-paxtons-death-9934233

Last time we were together was at screening of my film "Cannes Man." I didn't talk to you, but I heard your distinct laugh in the audience. How'd you like that film?

When you said, "I didn't talk to you" he said, "I did talk to you."

That's correct, yes, when I called you up to invite you. (Ding!) We did speak on the phone. Sorry, I forgot.

When you said, "How'd you like the film?" He feels so much like - you and he wanted to do something similar or that you did similar work – it seems like he saw himself in it.

> (Note: As noted, Bill and I tried to work together on *"You Can't Hurry Love."* It starred Bridget Fonda and David Packer. When he made *"A Simple Plan"* he called to tell me "I finally got to work with Bridget!" *"Cannes Man"* was about a hapless delivery boy who comes to the film festival, and just using hype turns into the "flavor of the moment." Bill and I also spent a few fun evenings in Cannes together over the years. He absolutely could have played the part.)

Rich: He should have been in it.

Kimberly: He feels like it (the story) **represents him...**

Billy I just wanted to open this door, I thought this would be a fun chance to say hi.

He says... It's funny it feels like he's such a smart aleck! He says, "You always have a chance to say hi, you don't need *her*." He's very funny.

I'm just seeing if I can help you in some way to connect with your loved ones, and don't hesitate to stop by. Let me ask, so were you impressed when we spoke to Jesus a few moments ago?

> (Note: Just prior to my asking questions, I asked Kimberly about her visions where she has seen Jesus during some of her mediumship sessions, and we spoke about her journey to this work. I segued from "talking to Jesus" to asking him to bring forward "my pal Bill.")

He's razzing you. He says... um, he's like "What are you talking about, Jesus and I, we go way back, what are you talking 'bout?" He's like "Where are *you*?" He's kind of beating you up.

> (Note: She could not possibly know that's our relationship. Glad to hear he's still enjoying the mutual razzing.)

So Billy, when you're looking at us in this restaurant in West Hollywood, what do you see?

He looks at watch, he's like looking at his watch... did he smoke?

I don't remember. He may have.

It's like he's got a cigar, something bigger than a cigarette.

Tell him he's very missed.

He feels like the kind of guy... it's like "He knows no stranger," that kind of person (well loved).

That's accurate. So what's the biggest thing you learned passing over?

"That there is no time, there is no death." He didn't realize how much fear he had until he died, until he came here. "There is no fear; there is no time."

Did you have your past life review already?

He says, "A long time ago."

> (Note: A "past life review" is something that's common among people who have near death experiences, but it's also in the reports from people under deep hypnosis. I've filmed 45 sessions, done 5 myself and examined thousands from Dr. Helen Wambach and Michael Newton. People talk about "seeing their council" and then having a review of all the good or bad things they've done in their lifetime.)

Any of the highlights... (laughs) or low lights you want to share? Anything you were surprised to see?

(Kimberly aside) Wow, that's an interesting perspective. **He says that he realizes... he says...** I'll just say it verbatim as if I'm him; **"I'll say this. I realize the fear that I carried within myself planted fear in others and for that I shed remorse. I acknowledge my remorse and I know I have to heal in that way." He's showing** (me) **the collateral damage he did, he's giving an example; here's an example; "If we walk around** (during our lifetime) **saying "I'm so worried," like "I'm so worried about my heart** (or other fears) **because then we believe in our fears." And it created this collateral damage. He didn't realize how**

much he did that. Like he "Just worried about stuff that was minute," he says.

So how'd you like your memorial service?

He stood up and did a salute.

Some of your friends have written some wonderful tributes on Facebook. Are you aware of them?

No, it feels no connection. He says to tell you that he can connect emotionally to his friends, like when it goes to social media it has an emotional imprint; but it's almost invisible to them (on the flipside)."

Is there any one thing you want me to tell you friends and fans?

He's funny. I really like his personality; he's one of those people who's going to give you a little bit... just enough to make you want more. **When you said, "Is there anything you want me to tell your friends and family?" He literally said, "I can fly."** (Kimberly laughs) **He's playing the song "I can fly, I can fly"...** (The Peter Pan version). **He's laughing because it's like, "I know they want more... but this is what I'll give them: I can fly."**

(Note: This is the same thing he said to Jennifer.)

Can you tell Kim your last name?

Kimberly laughs. (to Bill: "Why?" She then gestures with a "zipped lip.") **That's what he did. I said, "Are you sure?" He's checking his pockets** (as if looking for a wallet.) **He said "Nope." He zipped his lip and then pointed to you.**

225

I have other friends named Billy who are on the other side, just to be sure, tell her which one of my Billy's is this? (trying to trick him into revealing it to her.)

He said, "Whichever one had the heart issues." Now he's pulled his energy back.

(Note: There's only one who had heart issues.)

We ended the interview, and then moments later Kim's father called from Ohio to see how she was doing on her trip out West. She asked him what he was doing and she later said; "He told me he was watching this old film called "Twister."

At that point I told her who Bill Paxton was, and how he was the star of that film. She was surprised, but not as much as I was at the clever way he revealed his identity to her. I mean *"What are the odds?"*

All I can say is *"Well played, Bill. Well played."*

*****

Dennis Hopper and Luana in "Night Tide."

CHAPTER ELEVEN:

BILL FROM TEXAS PART II

"I love him."

Young Bill and his 16mm camera

I reached out to a friend of Bill's on Facebook – another actor who he had worked before. I told him about our conversations and he wrote in an email:

"Please send him my love (and tell him) **"The buddhas are unscathed and have a laugh at the "Thai cocksman's" expense. Tell him I miss riding bikes in the middle of the night."**

The next time I saw Jennifer, I brought this email up directly to Bill.

*****

Rich: Class, who's here?

Jennifer: They're all saying "I, I, I..."

*It's all about **you**! So Luana, how are you?*

She said she's been here (waiting) for 2 hours.

People are talking about you Billy. I got this feeling I should sign onto Facebook and there was a photo of Bill and a mutual friend wrote "I'm missing my friend." I sent him a private message, telling him about our conversations with Bill. He wrote back, essentially saying "Thank you, I'm into this."

Wow. Bill just got mad at me – "Stop being a skeptic," he said.

He had a couple of things to pass you along, Billy.

Bill showed me a letter, as in "I got the letter." (Jennifer aside) I still don't know how to see "email" – they just show me a letter. **He's saying, "I got the mental mail."**

Rich: He had three things he referred to, I can read it to you or have you guess its content. What do you prefer?

Jennifer: Billy wants me to try to get it. He's showing me boxes?

Correct. He referred to a gift.

Something to do with time... like a watch?

I don't think it's a watch, but perhaps to do with time.

Oh, he's showing me that his friend's child came back to him.

That is correct too. Bill has a friend whose child was missing. Did you help him with that reunion?

"Everyone did." I asked him, "Did you have to or did it work itself out?" **He's saying "No, everyone had to work it out, work on it."**

How did you help?

"He put their awareness where it needed to go." Like the penny issue; they make it seem like there no pennies on the floor, and then put your awareness towards seeing them there. They just gave me a high five (for that answer).

Is the family okay or are they working on issues?

"Working on issues."

Who said that?

All of them. They showed me all the people behind Billy, and everyone else is thinking and their reply is like a flash in his mind.

What issues are they working on?

His friend's child was born a boy and changed to a girl.

    (Note: This is correct.)

Jennifer: That's what the father can't believe.

*Rich: **Accept** or believe?*

Accept. (She taps her nose for "correct") He's trying really hard.

Should I try to explain to his friend this research that claims we choose our incarnations?

"Yes."

Okay, that's a tough conversation, I'll see what I can do.

They aren't done with their answer yet. **He needs to find out why he won't accept it. Could be because of a past lifetime, understanding that connection.**

> (Note: People in this research claim that we choose our lifetimes. That we may often choose one gender, and then come to the planet and feel unresolved, as if we hadn't thought it through to pick a lifetime with a different gender than we normally pick. Either way it's a choice, and we eventually realize why we made that choice.)

That would be a way of resolving it in this lifetime?

"Yes." High five. (Meaning she's seeing people on the flipside giving us high fives for the answer.)

Let's deal with his questions for Billy from his friend the actor; Donal Logue. Donal wrote about something that is unscathed that are objects. Bill, can you put in Jennifer's mind an image of what these objects are?

He went like this (gestures) **like a picture.**

Could be a sculpture or painting of someone or something... religious in nature. I don't know.

He's showing me a painting, a memoir of somebody's life. **He's saying, "It relates to something... a virgin."** He

showed me a movie. He's showing me a painting of virgins... I feel like like some expression about virgins.

That's correct. He's referring to himself as a guy who slept with a lot of women "Have a laugh the Thai cocksman" he says.

That's where the virgin comes from. He's joking because he was the opposite.

He wrote, "The Buddhas are unscathed. Are those statues or a painting?

(Laughs) **I'll just say it; I just got a pair of boobs. Like the Buddhists are anatomically correct.**

I think this cocksman reference is that everyone on the set was whoring around, but Donal was not.

"He was a virgin there but not anywhere else." Billy is saying, "His friend is a hypochondriac who doesn't want to get his hands dirty." They're all laughing. "Those humans."

Are the buddhas a gift painting or statues?

Oh my god! (Jennifer laughs) **Please tell me it's not that.** The buddhas... have penises. Unscathed... like they're not circumcised? **It also has something to do with movies.**

They did a movie in Thailand together, so maybe that's it.

Feels like he sent him a script about a movie.

He writes "Tell him that I miss something we used to do in the middle of the night."

I saw him telling him like a joke at night... feels like they were having conversations.

While they were having these conversations, they were doing something. Put it in her mind Billy.

I get working out... running?

No.

Bicycling? He's showing me bicycle riding... having a conversation at night, riding around.

Billy show her what you guys did when you rode.

He's showing me a map, a mountain road...

Where? Near Bill's home?

That feels like it.

So you're riding around at night in Ojai? Just having a conversation?

They're talking about places to film.

Bill, give her a detail from those conversations... what did you talk about? "Is this a good place to film a movie?"

(Jennifer laughs.) **I got that they had a sleepover – they had the same taste in women. Lots of jokes. Talking about a future project – talking about films.**

Bill was writing and directing his own films by that time, is that right?

Jennifer taps her nose. (Yes) **I just got shown that movie in Italy that Billy went to visit, like a foreign location. Something outside the US.**

> (Note: When Jennifer saw *"Just Call Me By Your Name"* she was surprised to see it dedicated to him at the end of the film. Apparently, he had stopped by the set to visit on the way to the Cannes film festival.)

I think this will be helpful to your buddy, Donal, if there's something that resonates with him. What were they doing in the dream?

Playing ball. Throwing a ball in the dream.

Maybe he'll remember that part of it.

> (Note: Donal Logue's email said: "Please send him my love- the buddhas are unscathed- and have a laugh at the "Thai cocksman's" expense tell him I miss riding bikes in the middle of the night.")

*****

I sent Donal a transcript of the above session. *His reply*:

Regarding: Bike riding

"That's incredible. We'd ride bikes at night and talk about a film called "The Yellow Mill Pond" that we knew we'd have to make in Hungary or Bulgaria."

re: "Thai Cocksman" and "Buddhas"

"Yes, I was chaste in Thailand. That is very specific. We bound buddhas together and shipped them back home.

The art and the anatomical jokes about a piece of art are on point." Finally, he added; "Intense. Wow. I love him."

>(Note: I wasn't going to mention Donal's name, but Bill insisted that I do so in this chapter.)

*Hey class, can we talk about **intercession**? From your perspective, if someone wants you to intercede on their behalf – knowing your higher self doesn't want or need the help, or that the person actually asked for their guides not to help so they could "Really learn the lesson" - how's that work? Do you guys argue with the higher self? Or do you somehow already know the answers?*

"They have boundaries."

Talk to us about the boundaries. Who created them?

"Like the movie "Coco.""

The bridge, that's a boundary?

"You have to know the boundaries."

Anyone else?

My dad, Jim. He's saying, **"You get it."** He knows I've been doubting every day – I doubt it with him... This class has made it easier for me to connect... this class makes it easier.

Why is this class making it more effective? Please show her the energy of how her work helps make it easier.

I see an image of light coming from behind your head... all of that energy coming together.

What can you share that you want us to know?

We talked about how everything seems to be slowing down, just this morning, we were talking about how the day is super slow and they showed me everything slowed down. It was like a had... what do you call that?

An epiphany?

Yes. Like (pulling up to) **a stop sign – they made it all slow down.**

I don't understand.

They made time slow down for us here – which allows everyone to connect elsewhere...

People need to slow down time to connect?

Slow it down so spirit can communicate. You need to create that space, and when you feel that time is slowing down... ask questions. Like, "Why is this happening? What do I need to know?"

The way we do in class; we let time slow down, find the space to connect and go from there?

"Yes." There's applause for that comment. Every time we meet with our class, there's something so valuable that comes from this... it's fascinating – everything is going around them, all the chaos. They get thoughts that are projected to them from their loved ones.

But by slowing our energy down, like approaching a stop sign, we become more aware of our surroundings, our spirits, and by the time we get to the stop sign, they connect to us.

"Visualize yourself and the environment around you in slow motion..." they showed me super slow motion where everything stops. **"No matter what's going on around you, (when) you allow your focus to slow down... you slow down, and at the moment of stopping you can ask the questions to your loved ones."**

You stop and they say "go?"

"Stop. Connect. Go."

(Laughs) As opposed to "turn on, tune in, drop out."

Jennifer; aside: I can't make this shit up! **He showed me a stop sign... okay what does that mean? Now I understand it, he just gave that to me – they did.**

So a stop sign is a valuable way to help people to access their loved ones. Picture the stop sign, slow everything down, and then connect to your loved ones. Thanks Class.

Luana and Dennis Hopper in "Easy Rider"

CHAPTER TWELVE:
P. ROGERS NELSON
"Surfing the Ethers"

"Home." Photo Courtesy NASA

As noted, Prince has shown up a number of times during our conversations. I mentioned the following conversation in *"Hacking the Afterlife."*[44]

*Richard: So **why is the veil thinning?** Why is that thing between us becoming easier to access?*

---

[44] Reprinted from *"Hacking the Afterlife"* Createspace publishing 2016. With permission from myself.

Jennifer: (Robin) just showed me Prince.

Prince the musician? What about him?

I don't know.

He's in the new book. (I was still working on it.)

Is he? Give me a second… **When you said, "why is the veil thinning," he showed me Prince**. (Pause, listening.) He said, "Prince just wanted to go home."

What?

"Prince just wanted to go home."

Okay I understand. I include an interview with him in the book. In the interview, he talks about what it was like when he got home.

Yeah.

Are you guys friends? (Robin and Prince) You guys hang out?

(Laughs.) They're both laughing. **"We go way back."** They're laughing about the whole concept of "way back." Like *what does that mean?* In their world, where they're at, way back is like… (laughs).

Let me ask Prince a question. Are you aware of your (chapter) in my book?

….He's showing me reading a book. Page 149. (or 49).

What's he reading?

I don't know. (pause) **He says you're at not taking things out.** He's laughing; he says, "It's a good thing." I asked (him)

238

"Is it a good or a bad thing?" And he gave me a look, said "It's a good thing."

You mean not taking things out... you mean like I'm allowing everything to be in?

Yes, everybody else takes bits and pieces out. .... He says, **"Love is what it is."** Now he's playing his guitar.

....So, Prince what are you and Robin up to?

"Surfing the ethers."

Surfing the ethers? Cool. Do you go around and check out your fans, reach out to them? Or do you guys hang around and do your own thing?

(Listens) No, what? (Laughs. Nods. Smiles.) They're both teaching (the class) **"How Not to Leave the Earth Early."**

Excellent, well that's a great class. I'd like to take that class. I know a few people who need to take that class.

....He says "Music hurts too much;" it hurt his joints. He said, **"It hurts."** ..... They said, **"Thank you for not questioning our existence... from your guides."**

....How about Prince, any last words?

"Live and let live." [45]

*****

So it's not an odd thing when Prince Rogers Nelson shows up in our conversation.

---

[45] Excerpted from "Hacking the Afterlife"

Rich: Ok, so we had a question for someone in our class. Who's here?

Jennifer: Prince is here. He really wants to answer the question. *By the way I'm asking, "Is this really Prince?"*

Okay, that's good, because I know this woman who had 3 near death events, and when I told her about our conversations, she said she wanted to ask Prince a question. I was watching him dance a few days ago.

Jennifer: "That was old stuff," he said.

> (Note: That was accurate. Footage from him rehearsing "Purple Rain.")

I think it's cool they're finally putting out your work.

He said, "It's about time."

Well you were "Mr. Secretive..."So what do you think about them releasing your new old material?

He said, "They're not going to get the ending right."

Do they ever?

Everyone's laughing.

There is no ending.

Everyone's laughing when you said that. They're reminding me of the flat tire – how Harry Dean thought the afterlife was a dream, but then when he got the flat tire realized he couldn't be in a dream.

Okay, I need us to give Jennifer a recap of the stop sign conversation we had before... Kind of confusing. How does slowing things down help us access the flipside?

"First you can't text and drive." **That's funny** (To the class: "I heard you loud and clear." Jennifer puts up two hands) **Originally, it was like I didn't know when my dad was communicating with me, he showed me going to a stop sign and consciously stopping your thoughts so that you can access new ones. You know how we go around driving unconsciously, it's a meditative state? He's saying...** "When you arrive at a stop sign it slows everything down and it's then you ask, "Who's here?" And see what comes in."

This woman I met at a dinner party had a question for Prince. She says she felt she had a conversation with you the day you died. Was that accurate or imaginary?

"It was not imaginary but..." he's holding up his finger – **"She was tapping into the matrix of what was happening. It wasn't that they were having a conversation - it's not like he came to visit her - but it's like there's a big bandwidth and she tapped into the bandwidth. It's such a big bandwidth, whoever is dialing in can get into the same phone call... so if something is happening and she's dialed in, she can access that matrix, she was online with what was happening with him."**

Not because she's tuned into his frequency, but because she's a fan of his, and was able to access that frequency?

"Her subconscious accessed what was happening to his frequency."

Sounds as if whoever is tuned a particular way can feel "there's a disturbance in the force." She says she asked you questions, wanted to know if it was really you answering.

He showed me the matrix of him; the frequencies of who he is.

She wondered if was important information for her future...

He said, "Don't try to make something out of it, just allow it."

Does he mean me or her?

"Her. Her subconscious made that event, where she felt herself in an enclosed space, her mind made that seem as if that was the elevator where they found him." I had something similar when I got an image of something bad happening to Prince, and then saw a plane going down... saw him in a jet.

That was a few days before, when they had to land his plane after his Atlanta performance for a drug overdose. Okay, let me ask Prince, this... we spoke 6 months ago, what does that feel like to you in terms of time?

A thousand years. He showed me a vast sea of lights...

When people pray or think of you, do you respond to everybody? Are you enjoying that or is that work?

He just hit you upside the head like that was a rhetorical question... **He says, "He's not helping them; he's igniting them."**

Igniting?

He showed me a flame, getting it to spark; that's what I'm seeing.

Like literally lighting their inner matches?

He showed me a musician, putting in their mind they can work, they can play, sparking them.

Is that something you learned to do over there; is this a new quality?

He did it before but didn't know he was doing it – it's always been his role to spark people; he didn't know it was the case when he was here.

You're inspiring people to be creative?

It's a combination – but he's saying, "a more powerful word than combination." He's got a powerful connection with the people who consider him a spark. He's showing me Whitney.

Houston? You're hanging out with her?

He's calling it "the *black brat pack*."

Who else is there?

He's saying her daughter.... and Sammy Davis Jr.

Do you guys perform together?

He says, "They're practicing for their next lives." Hold on. Okay, from what I'm getting: **"You create your life up there. You're busy talking to people, working with people, and you come down there and you're supposed to remember it."** (What you practiced.)

Well we all take a swig of "forget-me-juice" before we arrive. So let's say you're training to be an athlete, a football player, sniper or surgeon. You're honing your craft before you come here and you get to a point during your life, hopefully, where you get to practice your craft. Is that correct?

"Yes."

Very cool. Anyone else?

They're all raising their hands.

Who wants to talk?

Robin.

Hey there's a documentary coming out about you – someone who loves you made it.

"Magical," he says. His family is really involved in this, feels like.

So your review is "It's magical?"

"Magical but not the beginning. It builds up the story."

What's the beginning about?

"His parents."

They're trying to rationalize why you took your own life?

"They talk about cocaine (in the show)."

Is it inaccurate or not the whole picture?

"Just not the whole picture. They shouldn't emphasize the struggle as much." Robin showed me the homeless guy.

244

"Radioman?" The character he played in "The Fisher King" with Jeff Bridges?

"Hollywood's like that; they just do that."

"Conflict is the essence of drama..." we could ask Aristotle to come in and give us that lecture, but we won't.

He's giving me goose bumps. I love that... "Conflict is the essence of drama." An "OxyMormon" my dad just said.

OxyMormon? That's hilarious.

My dad said to me "You are conflict." How everybody is in conflict with themselves, you have to give people permission (to be who they are) – **that's what I learned from him.**

Your dad is calling you an Oxymoron or an OxyMormon? Nobody laughed at that?

Luana did.

Thanks Lu. Here's my question... I've been telling people that based on our research we only bring about a third of our conscious energy to the planet, roughly, and when we access the other two thirds, can we ask them questions like we ask you?

Your higher self?

Yes, but the higher self of someone who is currently incarnated on the planet. In other words, someone I know - can we ask their higher self questions? Is that possible? Or inappropriate?

There has to be a connection of some sort.

Sure, someone we know.

I could ask if I can bring them forward. (A pause) **"For medical reasons,** (they're telling me) **Yes."**

But not for the "Rich Martini show?"

"Yes, but within reason – they'll give us the idea to do it or not."

I'm asking because it could be helpful to people, could be a health issue. Like asking "How can we help you recover form the illness you have, whether in real time, with us, or by way of information?"

Hang on... (Jennifer listens). It's the same with me getting something physically; "As long as there is a connection." It's what I do... they're showing me "that's a possibility."

By me asking questions...

As long as they are open to it... hold on. "You have to ask permission." I'm asking, "Can we do that, speak to their higher self about an illness?" and they're saying, "No, you have to ask permission."

Some things are not permissible to pass along, as it would interrupt or disrupt their path?

I always ask for permission when it comes to passing along information about someone's health. Just because they say it is, doesn't mean I should pass it along. For example, I had a friend's relative in a coma, this person told me details about everyone in the room. I asked if he was going to make it, and he said "My spirit is fighting but my body might not allow me to come back in." So I told them that.

I met a woman from Australia whose brother was in a coma. She told me a masseuse friend doing work on her brother, she kept hearing her brother in her head saying, "yellow goggles." The woman realized they'd left blinds up because he was "brain dead;" the bright sun was in his eyes, and he was asking for his ski goggles. So she put them on him.

I'll ask the person in a coma to give me a visual of "where you are when you're not struggling." And they'll say, "I'm in a forest, near a waterfall," and then the family can always think of them when they see that.

Luana, I need your help bringing someone forth. Both you and my mom knew her.

They're showing me the fish Dory.

Well yes, that's her name; Doreen. (ding!)

She's already here. She's fixing your hair.

She was close to my brother.

> (Note: Doreen Tracy, one of the original Disney Mouseketeers.)

Did she have breast cancer?

Yes. (Ding!) She passed two or three weeks ago, has a son.

He's tall.

Doreen, tell Jennifer about the woman who gave you some money, this young girl you helped...

I saw Monte Carlo... when this girl was younger, her parents weren't around so Doreen kind of took her in.

(Ding!) Can you show Jennifer what your occupation was?

Somewhere in California, I'm getting... like an agency...

> (Note: That's accurate, she worked as an agent and as a secretary at Warner Brother's music.)

She was part of a troupe of performers... that's when Doreen helped this young girl who later helped her.

And then I get troops. Did she perform for the troops?

I don't know.

> (Note: Something I was not aware of; I found online that she had toured extensively in Vietnam. *Ding!)* [46]

She was a performer.

On TV?

Yes... associated with a group...

Disney? Oh my god.

Yes, she was a Mousketeer. She also worked at Warner Records, worked with Frank Zappa and others... a generous soul. Anything you want to pass along to my brother?

---

[46] "Doreen Tracy ...toured Vietnam with the USO. Trading her formerly demur Mouseketeer sweater & ears for a skin-tight t-shirt, white go-go boots and mini-skirt, Tracey was choppering from base to base as she entertains the troops. Performing covers of then-popular 1960s songs like "Hold On, I'm Coming" and "We've Gotta Get Out of This Place" with her band, Doreen and the Invaders." https://www.huffingtonpost.com/entry/looking-back-at-the-colorful-show-business-career-of_us_5a5d36aae4b01ccdd48b5ef6

She says that "He sees her. She said that everything's gonna be okay."

He told me he had a dream about her before her death.

They were holding hands, there was a flower involved, like he gave her a flower. She showed me they were very happy, I don't know if there was a truck or a barn or something in the country.

(Note: My brother says this is accurate.)

Any advice for my brother?

He's right about already seeing her in person, and to not discount that. Bill Paxton just came up to my ear.

What do you want to say buddy?

Bill says "Tell Rich that I'm working with him. Finally."

I'm sure that was cool for your pal to talk to you. He loves you. Okay guys, thank you. Nice chatting with you. Thanks Doreen. Thanks class.

The adorable Doreen Tracy

CHAPTER THIRTEEN:

P. R. NELSON PART II

"Don't lose the attachment."

Luana with her pal Michael Gough

This photo above was *kismet*.[47] Luana and I were backstage at Michael "Mick" Gough's Broadway play "Breaking the Code." We asked to see him, but no one gave him the message. So we wandered backstage, and while walking across the pitch black stage, Luana bumped into him in the dark. Pitch black and he and Luana found each other. I took this photo moments later.

---

[47] Arabic word for "Fate"

They had been friends since they both appeared on Broadway when Luana was a teen (with Rex Harrison in "Der Luberlu" directed by Peter Brooks) Mick and Luana remained the best of pals over the decades.

Seven years after her passing, I was in Tibet camped in a tent on the side of Mt. Kailash. I heard Mick's voice, clear as a bell in my tent saying "Richard, I think what you're doing is fantastic!" I was startled – I had no idea if he was alive or dead, but clearly it was his voice.

I said in my head "Mick? Is that you? Are you dead?" And he said, "No darling, occasionally I take trips with Luana around the universe and I just stopped by to say that what you're doing is simply marvelous." I had the impression that our friend Luana was hovering some distance away as to not interfere.

When I finished the journey around Kailash, I found an internet cafe in Darchen, a small village at the foot of the sacred mountain. I emailed Mick's wife Henrietta... "How is Mick? Is he okay?" The email I got back from her was "Oh, he's fine. He's napping right now." I couldn't figure out how to write what had happened in an email. It took me a year to get him on the phone so I could pass it to him directly. I was in transit in Heathrow when I rang him up.

I told him the story, and asked "Have you ever had a dream where you were traveling around outer space with Luana?" And he said, "No darling, but it sounds absolutely fantastic!" After Luana passed, I had made a point of visiting him and his lovely wife Henrietta, and scattered some of Luana's ashes around the bench in the back of their home that overlooked the English countryside. I like to think that he's continuing his adventures with Luana, as he's no longer on the planet.

Something I'll have to explore in a future session with Jennifer. But this photograph reminds me that we "never lose the connection that is between us."

*****

Rich: We were going to talk about healing... so Luana, as we all know, I've been in your classroom and I've talked to your teacher in your class about the healing process... I've asked about the healing process which includes altering the future – there is no such thing as healing unless there's illness?

Jennifer: Correct. Morton just arrived.

Okay, Michael Newton – Morton - we were now going to address the topic of healing individuals here on the planet.

He's showing me so many...

Including how to heal people who may not want to be healed so they can learn that energetic lesson.

I was just shown something that actually hurts. I was shown my dad. That if he would have lived longer we wouldn't have been able to work together with him the way we are working together now. I wouldn't be able to learn from him on the other side. Because it's a different learning when it's coming from him on the other side.

Are you saying it's impossible to alter others' paths without their help?

No. They just showed me a quick preview of when my dad, when he passed... Now they're trying to make me laugh...

showing me the baby Jesus, which was my nickname for him (As in "He could "do no wrong."") He was an only child, perfect in everyone's eyes... He's showing me that, yeah, the power of prayer, **the power of that frequency is the power to heal.**

The power of prayer is the power of that frequency to heal?

"However that looks; to the gods, goddesses... you have to call on it from all lifetimes."

For example, if you were going to pray for some individual we perceive as ill, unhappy - how would we call upon the healing light of the universe in order to assist this person we think needs help?

"We have to change the way our hearts view him or her in order to help them."

So the first order of business is we alter our perception of reality as to who we think that person is?

"Correct. We make him or her just a human being."

Think of him or her as a person with a soul. Then how do we call upon the healing light of the universe to help?

It's important that you have to believe in the power of prayer, and I'm seeing as an example, Dwayne Johnson's avatar in the film "Jumanji" – in truth we are all much bigger elsewhere. And we can send that frequency from all parts of it to the person in need of healing. We can call upon the angels.

So if you're going to ask for the healing light, shift your perception of that person, then connect yourself to your higher consciousness?

That's key. Take a "bad person" for example; it's the attachment we have of him as a temporary being. We have to lose the attachment to who they are in order to give the medicine to them. We don't know what they're like elsewhere.

So when we unlock or open our hearts and connect to our higher consciousness?

They showed me... if I'm giving medicine for this place or person, but I detach from that, open my heart - then I can give medicine through prayer. And whatever I do in this process, it becomes medicine for him or her everywhere.

There are the two thirds of his higher energy we can access... (seeing her wince) What's the matter?

Ow, this hurts. It's really weird.

Are you getting some kind of download? Or is someone disagreeing with this assessment?

Hold on. Wow. (Jennifer laughs) They're saying you don't have to do a detachment, that is a metaphor – it's (just) to realize there's so much more.

Who disagreed with you?

My dad.

So Jim you put a pain in your daughter's head to get her attention?

He didn't do it, it's the frequency of not getting it right. That really hurt by the way – normally it's a high pitch, they put a high pitched pain on my side... **Our friend Prince just showed up to weigh in on this; showed me the film "Coco" and said, "Don't lose the attachment."**

Because in his case, Prince's music is everywhere and people access him that way... **it's not about our detaching ourselves from someone else, or about an attachment, they want us to know that there's so much more, infinitely more. Nobody is really aware of that, because they're looking at just this life.**

To recap; it's a bit like the Tibetan meditation called Tonglen which means "Give and take." You picture your loved one in a happy state, then imagine their illness as a color or smoke, pull it out of them and into you and then to ask the healing light of the universe to transform that into a healing energy before you breathe the healed energy back into them. Something like that?

The whole class is behind you on that... but your heart has to be clearly immersed without the attachment to the outcome. Meaning, even if someone dies here...

They don't die over there.

Hang on. **"Even though you might die here, it doesn't mean it didn't help them elsewhere – they might die here, but their energy might be rebuilt (healed) elsewhere."**

They may not be healed here, but they are healed on some level somewhere else?

Luana is saying "yes" and showing me my muscles – we don't know how powerful we are, because we don't allow

ourselves to realize how strong we are. Bill Paxton showed up.

So Billy – you appeared in Jennifer's consciousness – as the film she just saw "Call Me By Your Name" is dedicated to you... your agent's husband produced the movie, and Bill had gone to visit the set in Italy, and the director decided to dedicate the film to him.

He's showing me the guy, the guy that the boy fell in love with...

Armie Hammer.

He had a connection in helping with his character –

Ok.

But it was unanimous that they dedicate the film to him.

What else, Billy?

He's showing me the anniversary of his passing is coming around. I don't remember.

It's coming up, yeah, February (this is January.)

He just showed me the 14th or 24th of Feb.

(He passed on the 25th) You want me to post anything?

His voice is so great. Hang on. **"That they're working really hard over there. They're in charge of the coincidences of everything happened here – they're the master minds of that."** Why did he show me the film "Avatar?"

He knows the director.

256

Right. He's making you meet him. And then you'll know. That will be interesting.

Do you have any message for Jim Cameron?

There's a dream he had in November about Bill. They played football – he showed me a movie with a football, something to do with that sport?

Does Jim remember the dream?

It will be "foggy," he says.

Is there anyone that you know Billy that would help Jim know it's you?

It felt like Jim mentored someone close to him, who was like a son to him, who passed away, feels like cancer... I got something way long ago – 1989.

That could be very specific – someone Jim knew, felt like a son, died of a cancer in 1989, Bill brought that up so that Jim would know it's Bill reaching out to him?

"Yes."

Anyone in our group who wants to speak up?

Your mom.

Hi mom. Anthy, what do you want to say?

Your son is doing great. She showed me he's doing creative things you can't see. Was there a performance last night?

I had our son perform a piano piece on Facetime for his godfather, Charles Grodin. (ding!)

She said it was fantastic. She's always with him, they were all there.[48]

Anything my mom wants to tell my brothers?

"Love. Know that they're loved. They don't always feel that way. You are loved, you can't feel that way about yourself but know you are loved." She's showed me like a shooting star, tons of pink light, it's a loving color.

Love yourself because...

"You'll be able to feel love. If you don't recognize what it feels like you can't know it." Your mom is a calming influence. She says, "Thank you."

For what?

"For opening up your mind. Your heart has always been open but opening up your mind..." – the whole class... it's like they're giving you a standing ovation.

Take a look at Mom. How old does she appear you?

I want to say 89. That's what comes up.

That's correct.(Ding!)

She was 89, she says. Bright eyes, same as your son, same kind of intensity, not color... – did she work in the garden a lot?

---

[48] Dorothy Ann Martini (Anthy) was a concert pianist, played about an hour every day up until her last day on the planet. Videos of her playing at AnthyMartini.com

In her youth, I once asked her to describe heaven and she described living in a "comfy home with a garden."

She's making everything grow.

I called her to tell her a close friend died, and instead of saying "Paul Tracey died" I said, "Mom, what do you think heaven is?" She said, "I feel like it's a reproduction of your home, a place you create where you feel comfy, surrounded by the people, trees and garden you love." Which turned out to be what I've learned in this research. I was surprised; I thought she would have said something "more Catholic."

She's got her garden.

Paul Tracey is a guy who's showed up in class.

> (Note: I mention in the book "Flipside" how I was walking with difficulty around Mt. Kailash, and I heard his voice saying "You think it's hard for you? Imagine me!" (He had his hip replaced when we were in high school.) I was startled – had not been thinking about him. He said, "Thank you for the happiest day of my life." I didn't know he meant, then he showed me; a day in our teens when we got lost behind my uncle's house in Ohio and spent the day at a swimming hole.
>
> Later, I remembered I had the titanium ball from his hip in my suitcase. (His mom sent me some of his ashes, when I went to bring some on this trip, I found this steel ball in the ash, and realized it was from his hip. As our friend Dave Patlak put it "the thing Paul hated so much in life he willed to you." So when I found a giant stone stupa some days later, I put the

steel ball in the middle. Paul's hip is now holding up a stupa on the far side of Mt. Kailash in Tibet.)

Jennifer: She really liked him – maybe a little more than any one thinks.

Rich: Join the club. That's funny. Bless his heart. Cool.

(Note: Around Paul's birthday (May 4th) I got a phone call from our mutual friend. I mentioned that she had a dream where he sat with her and reminded her of the fun times they had together and said that he was sorry he didn't stay connected to her.

Then he said, **"Tell Richard I'm sorry I called him."** (new information) She called me to ask what that was about, and I reminded her that his last phone call was to me – I'd answered the phone annoyed, knowing that he was going to be drunk on a Sunday night, and said *"What?"* instead of *"Hello Pablo"* like I normally did.

I realized after he died that night that was his last phone call – and if I had called his parents and said something he'd still be on the planet. So, imagine my chagrin when last week, this mutual friend called and said "I was just in my AA meeting and I heard Paul's voice clear as a bell come through and say to me *"Tell Richard that it was my time. It was the time I was supposed to depart."* Important to stay open to messages that come through no matter where they come from.)

Jennifer: Richard, you dad just came through; he said, "I concur."

Rich: Ha! That reply is very much like him.

I wouldn't know that.

How about you, dad, what are you up to?

He's playing golf.

> (Note: Dad was an architect, many buildings in the Chicago area. Later he built the Sheraton in the Nile in Cairo, traveled the world with my mom. He was an artist as well, and pretty much charmed everyone he met. He rarely golfed because he was a lefty, and it was hard to find left handed clubs. He's the third person to mention golfing on the flipside; makes me wonder if it's a country club we have to pay dues to get into).

Oh, that's funny. He liked to golf but was left handed, so we had to find him left-handed clubs.

He says, **"The golf courses over there are infinite."**

Who do you golf with?

I'm seeing an African American.

Is that someone from your soul group?

"Yes. It's someone from Chicago," he says.

> (Note: I can only think of one family friend; his name was Kelly and he was friends with our family.)

Was it Kelly?

"Yes." (Jennifer aside) Who's that? Was he like a mayor?

Well on one level, yes. He was the only black person in our home town. He bagged groceries at the local grocery store, but was gracious to everyone. I was very fond of him, as he was one of the few adults who looked me in the eye when he spoke to me. When he retired, all three major papers in Chicago had him on the front page. I interviewed him recently, heard his life story. So yeah, like a Mayor of sorts.

His wife died recently.

I don't know. The town changed since then, Michael Jordan lived there for a while, and many of the Bulls and Bears.

I'm getting that it *is* Kelly.

>(Note: That's pretty funny. Dad was the assistant city architect for Chicago, on our town's Board of Trustees for 12 years and his strong regulations helped keep Northbrook, Illinois a classy suburb. Kelly was beloved by many and occasionally my dad asked him to tend bar for our neighborhood parties. Once Kelly had a "heavy hand" serving drinks and everyone was blotto by sundown. Kelly couldn't find his car keys, so everyone scoured the grass on hands and knees. Funny to see all the neighbors crawling around our yard drunk with flashlights. As an 11 year old, I asked myself "If I were Kelly's keys, where would I be?" I opened his car door, opened his visor and out they fell.)

Anyone else in our class? How about Prince? People were posting videos of him playing "Auld Lange Syne" at a New Year's eve party.

He's really busy... He's showing me Switzerland, but I feel like it's a metaphor for him being everywhere.

Like a neutral country?

A neutral state of being. But he's currently helping people cross over.

I'm sure that's fun for people crossing over the Flipside. "Oh my god, it's Prince!"

Purple Rain!

I was talking with a woman the other night, she said "I'm Jewish but I've had all these experiences with Jesus throughout my lifetime." She told me a few of them, and I told her how Jesus is non-denominational in this research. He shows up to a lot of different people!

He's very busy.

Of course Jesus is busy! Every Tom, Dick and Harry calling out his name whenever they can't think of a word. But is he too busy to talk to us?

No. But he's like "You got this already."

Jesus! What would you like me to tell people about running into you on the flipside?

"That I'm accessible." Everyone thinks "Oh, my God, it's Jesus!" That's the conundrum; people don't think they can talk to Jesus, but that is precisely why he comes through. He is accessible. You don't have to be privileged to have him in your life.

However, because of the way people perceive you, when they access you they go into a religious brain freeze. Jesus exists, so therefore every crazy thing my Catholic priest told me must be true. But that's not we're getting in this research.

If they thought of him as a color or light, they wouldn't have that.

But once they get a response from you...

"They discount it."

They fall into the biblical view – they go through "I'm not Christian, why am I seeing him?" I had another friend say Jesus appeared in a dream about his father, and when we did a session where he accessed it, he remembered meeting Jesus in the agora, market, buying cloth. But afterwards, this friend said to me "I'm Jewish! I don't believe in Jesus!" So once they hear from you how do they accept it is you?

"Belief."

But belief implies it might not be true. I hate to be arguing with you Jesus, but is there a better word? Let's say someone's praying to you, they're calling upon you and they hear back from you – you answer them. How can...

"In the way that you see others." So... if you're more in love with life, than that's him. "If you have compassion – that's him – it's what you see in other people," that is his response.

Let me see if I got this - let's say someone says a prayer to you and then your response is to have something come into their frame of reference that represents your response.

"Like a child runs up to them, someone who made them mad doesn't make them mad anymore... coming to them, or someone they didn't like changes their attitude and reaches out..."

The physical manifestation of you or your response, or your vibe will occur?

"In other people."

Can you give me a time frame? How soon can people expect a reply? A day, a week, or an hour - roughly?

"Instantly. Your heart will feel different."

So you'll open it to the person who has wronged you?

"You'll be getting more information about why that person behaved that way - your heart will change. You'll be getting more information as to why that person behaved like that, which causes compassion. It doesn't mean you have to... like forgiveness." *Isn't just to forgive them, but for us to let go.*

Okay, I'm saying give us a 1,2,3, a practice – if you pray for intercession on whatever it is – you make that prayer with your heart open and intercession will occur?

"Through frequency and through love."

Well through someone else... where you suddenly feel...

"Yes."

So when I pass this along to someone, where they ask if they can have something that will prove to them that he exists, that he has "answered their prayer...."

He just keeps showing me that it will occur through the eyes of someone else, whatever the thing is that you're doing – whatever gets lighter is how he shows up.

I get it – If you do change, it doesn't matter whether it's him or not – the effect is the same... what we're saying isn't that if you pray for someone's health for example, because of that person's reasons for becoming ill, he might not intercede, help a child walk across the street, not hate your grandmother or something, but on some level, he will intercede by helping you to open your heart to someone else. Is that right?

"Yes. You'll be an intercession for someone else."

Is there a term we can use for this – Christianity without using the religion – accessing Jesus without having to believe in a dogma or religion?

There is no word. I asked him "Love or faith?" And he said "No, the second you put something on it, (try to name it) **it diminishes what happens."**

Okay, we'll just call it "the Martini method." Catch you later, class!

Luana and Michael Gough, circa when they were on Broadway together

CHAPTER FOURTEEN:
RANDAL AND HARRY
"It's My Party"

Randal in front of the epic view from his home.

Some years ago, when Jonathan Krane was producing films, he produced a film directed by Randal Kleiser. Randal directed the most successful music film of all time ("Grease") and a number of great films. I met him at one of Sally Kellerman's parties, and saw more of him while he was making "*Getting It Right*" for Jonathan and MCEG.

His film *"It's My Party"* was based on a true story. Back in the early days of HIV infections, when someone got news that their "T cells had dropped;" death was certain to follow. Randal's ex partner was a handsome artist named Harry Stein, whom Luana and I were both fond of. We visited him in NYC once, ran into him later in L.A., we always enjoyed his quit wit and easy smile.

Some years after he broke up with Randal, Harry discovered his T cell count had dropped precipitously from his HIV infection and decided to have a "going away party" for himself.

I don't know the precise details of how that went down, but I know that Randal's film was about the event. It was a courageous film that starred Eric Roberts based on Harry's story of his party that ended with him using medicine for an assisted suicide.

I told Randal about my work with Jennifer and he was intrigued, and ultimately, we did a Skype session. I didn't tell Jennifer anything about Randal or his career; she didn't hear his last name until the day we did the session. Even then she didn't know anything about Randal's career, we did the session in real time and as you'll see, looked up his Wikipedia page after the session was over.

Jennifer is in front of her laptop, I'm filming her from the side, myself in a mirror. Only she can see Randal, but I can hear his voice and he can hear me.

*****

Jennifer: Can you hear me?

Randal: Hi. This is Randal. You must be Jennifer.

Jennifer: Yes. Hi Randal, how are you?

RK: I'm great. Is Richard with you?

Rich: I'm standing off to the side. All she knows about you is that your name is Randal... and she now knows you have a last as it's part of your Skype handle.

RK: Richard was talking about doing something about the afterlife in Virtual Reality... it would be a lot of fun to try to do something like that. I'm just getting familiar with the flipside; I know nothing about it.

Rich: (By way of explanation to Jennifer) Randal and I were talking about what we've been doing. Jennifer and I had just had a short conversation with Luana and asked her to stand by for our conversation.

RK: Wow.

Jennifer: Luana got mad at me for (missing) last week.

Rich: I think I told you this Randal – Jennifer and I get together and have these open discussions as if it's a classroom. Luana is the moderator in this construct– but we couldn't last week because of the holidays. That's around the same time that our mutual pal Sally Kellerman (Luana's oldest pal) called me about having lunch with you. Either amazingly coincidental or unique.

RK: Is time "real time" in the afterlife as it is here? Because if you're saying they're late, I kind of assumed they were floating around anytime anywhere.

Jennifer: What I try to do – Rich and I go the same restaurant every Thursday between 12 and 2 – I assume it's real time; but Rich made sure we would meet later today at 3. Luana put my awareness to the clock where I see it's 3:15, and I got the impression she was saying "We're late."

RK: I'm curious about how that works.

J: What I just got is that it's quantumly related – but hang on, because I don't believe that's a word. (Pause) Give me a second... interesting. There is no "real" time here or

there, but there is a moment in time where our frequencies are together and they're able to pick up on. If I'm hearing that right.

RK: Okay.

Rich: I think it's linear time over there, just relatively different. So different that 25 years here feels like ten minutes to them or so I've heard.

J: Like (life here is) a coffee stop.

Rich: Or I've heard that 100 years over here may feel like an hour to them.

(A high pitched squeal of feedback happens.)

J: There's someone trying to come through... hang on.

Rich: She's saying that someone is trying to come through... for Randal or for our conversation?

(Another high pitched squeaking.)

RK: Is that a sound coming from where?

Rich: I tried to research it; it sounds like when two open mics are together... It only happens during these sessions though.

RK: Is it on the phone or where is it coming from?

Rich: It could be the computer's mic feeding back – but for some reason I've heard it feed back when the energy shifts in the room while someone comes through to talk to Jennifer.

J: I can use Skype for my private sessions and that never happens... but when spirit comes through, I can't prove it,

but it has this feedback... like it's a different tone. (more squeaks)

RK: I can hear it.

J: (Pauses, listens) Randal, is there an anniversary of some sort with Christmas or in December for you?

RK: Yeah, there was a movie I did that was...

Hold on. Don't tell me any more because this is being presented as significant for you... just let me dive into organically because if you tell me, then I can't tell you.

You told me it was a movie. According to this person it was "a great piece of work. An amazing piece of work." I don't know if he's laughing about it, I don't know what that means... or why he would call it a masterpiece.

I think it's because... and it's my interpretation, and if I don't get it right, I just have to go back into it. But from what I'm getting it was a big event. He is adamant about the holidays and Christmas... and he's saying that it "blew up?"[49] (Listens) It was something very dear to his heart on many levels – does that make sense to you?

Yeah. Mmhm.

It was something you came back to every year or come back to every year.

I guess, yeah.

---

[49] Randal directed "Honey I Blew Up the Kids" – so it may be a reference to that.

271

Was there something five years ago? Could have been 25 years ago, give me a second. Related to the person I'm talking to.

> (Note: It was 25 years ago when Harry left the planet, and 23 years earlier when Randal made the film.)

Rich: Jennifer can you tell us what this person looks like to you?

He's wearing a jacket, like a leather jacket, his hair is not unruly... straight. I think he might have been bald later – I might be seeing two different people, hold on. (Pause) I feel like this is someone that was very connected to Randal.

Very connected.

He showed me a ring, so I don't know how that's connected, but you were connected in an agreement for marriage? I don't know.... he loved you Randal.

Rich: What's this person's first name if he can give it to us?

He just showed me the credits of a movie. I don't why.

Rich: You mean he showed you his name in the credits of a movie? That's a possibility. Randal has this person's name ever appeared in the credits of a movie?

RK: Yes.

J: He was really funny, he seems like a smartass. I don't know what he means by that, but he's funny.

RK: Who was there to greet him upon his return?

J: Give me a second... a lot of people did. A lot of musicians he was aware of... does that make sense to you Randal?

RK: There's a composer that we both know who has passed on...

J: Have I met Harry in the ethers? Another Harry?

Rich: Is that the name the name that comes to you?

J: Yes.

Rich: Harry. That's correct. Now we're specific who this person is.

> (Note. Jennifer didn't know anything prior to this session, so pulling up Harry's name is one of those "ding!" moments.)

J: He's showing me that he was very OCD – I don't know if he was a key in helping with directing, but he had very keen sense of how things should go. Very stubborn but had the biggest heart. Did he have a ring or some kind of jewelry that you exchanged?

RK: No.

Maybe a commitment? Hold on. His mother was the first one to greet him.

That's nice.

I wondered if it was his dad, but that didn't feel like a strong connection. Does that make sense?

I think his father is still alive.

Okay I'll leave that alone. Give me a second ... There are two dogs?

At least. Are their dogs up there?

One died right before or right after, like a year? Did you guys share a dog together?

Yes.

Did it travel everywhere with you guys? But it was treated like a child.

Yeah. Sort of.

I was also shown a horse.

There were horses.

> (Note: Randal lives on a ranch above Runyon Canyon. He owns and keeps horses there.)

Okay, he's showing me the number 3... 3 horses? Did he train horses? Who trained horses?

We had a trainer that trained us to ride them.

He's saying that was one of his happier moments. He loved that, was able to escape in his mind. I felt like he had a lot of pain in his upper back – either that or you did. Or he's showing me you're a pain in his back. Who is that you're connected to that has back or neck issues? Could be someone else coming in. Hold on. He's showing me hand written letters... Did he write you letters or a letter toward the end, or a script?

Could have been an agreement we had when we broke up.

It felt like it was amicable – I know there was a lot of hurt around the heart. He's showing me that it just didn't work out.

Can you ask him about the fire and how that happened?

I was shown the horses and was shown the fire – I just ignored it because we just had horses and fires here in southern California. He showed me a fire and the fear of the horses.

There was an amazing thing that happened after he died. There was a fire that helped me and I just wondered if he had anything to do with that.

I'm getting yes, but I need to give you evidence, so give me a second, okay? Did you see him through the fire as well? When you were looking at it did you feel him there?

No.

He's showing me being across from it, like if you were to see some, like the fiery...

I didn't notice him if he was there. (chuckles)

Rich: So you saw the fire, Randal?

RK: It was out when I got there (home). I just wondered if he started it, that's all.

Rich: Let's ask him.

Jennifer: He said he was involved with it. He keeps laughing about it, I can't get a straight answer from him. It was electrical correct?

RK: They couldn't figure out how it started...

I'm seeing the ceiling... it felt like it was electrical. I feel like he had something to do with it, (from the flipside) but I don't feel like he wants to take credit for all of it. Was it part of place that um... was it part of something that you were redoing?

Yes, that's correct.

It felt like it was a place that you were changing, and that you were redoing it and that's when it started... correct?

> (Note: Randal told me the Northridge Earthquake had damaged his home, he was worried about the cost of fixing it. And then the fire happened sometime later, and although his house nearly burned down he learned he was insured for it. Since the fire literally saved his house, he wondered if Harry had anything to do with that from the flipside.)

RK: Nobody knows how it started, the fire dept. couldn't figure out what started it... It was just happened to coincide with something that I needed done.

Rich: I think what he's saying is the thing that happened prior to the fire, that caused the problem, contributed to the electrical problem which caused the fire. Is that correct?

J: "Yes." He's also saying, "It could have been way way worse." He's saying, "It was very specific in the place where it happened."

RK: That's exactly right.

J: But he wants to say, "He was a "fire fighter" that made it better rather than starting it." He's saying, "He wanted

to take credit for being the fire fighter that helped stopped it."

RK: It stopped exactly at my bedroom.

Rich: How did you do that Harry? How do you stop a fire from the flipside?

J: He says, "He just brought everyone – it was a group thing."

RK: There were firefighters there, and it stopped at the place where I needed it to stop.

J: He's taking credit for that. I'm seeing that they helped the firefighters from over there.

RK: Then Harry's partner was the person I hired to rebuild on that spot. So he was helping both his partner and me.

J: He just winked. He's so funny... I can't wait to find out who he was.

RK: I have a question. Is he aware of the movie I made about the situation?

J: "Yes." He's showing me, him sitting in a director's chair. I don't know if that's what you do or if you're part of it... but he's saying, "You went overtime in the movie."

RK: I'm thinking about a project he did to honor him.

Rich: I think that's what we started with. I understood that to be what he meant when he was referring to the masterpiece.

RK: Oh, I see.

J: Yeah, that's it. The one that came out at Christmas time. He showed me how amazing that was and it was part of his heart and that it was a masterpiece... can you share with me the name of the movie?

RK: She doesn't know anything about you Randal. Randal made a small movie with friends about Harry's story called "It's My Party."

J: Wow. I'm talking to the person it was about and person who made it?

Rich: Harry do us a favor, would you help Jennifer see what's going on with Randal's life, journey or path; what he's up to.

J: Funny, he gave me some disheveled things at first, laughed and then gave me everything smooth that Randal has it under control. Something in July, like a deadline, something that you're doing... give me a second. Something with your thoughts last July and you started writing about or doing. There's a script.

RK: Well I'm writing a book; that could be it.

"And he's a chapter" he says... he's showing me a four – fourth chapter? He says his thoughts are part of that, you guys had a great energy together, a beautiful understanding of each other, he's showing me arms across arms. He's showing me you helped him with a deal of respect like no other partners did – he's saying that he loved your hair – he's showing me... do you have like an elbow pain?

Hip.

Okay, if I'm being shown that... give me a second. He's showing me this motion – opening up your arm. He's saying, "You still don't allow yourself to receive. You handle everything." He showed me your hand opening up but you still don't allow yourself to receive – in your mind you do, but your heart is rebellious and you're stubborn as well, but in a good way... He showed me you, Rich. You're able to ask the right questions but you let people come to their own conclusions.

Oh cool.

Without telling them what to do – but he's showing me that you listen... you listen with intent – most talk with intent, you listen with intent.

Rich: Randal and I were talking about this the other day; how an actor can teach you to "listen with intent."

RK: I learned it from (the actor) Scott Glenn. It's a way of acting like you're listening, but "listening with intent."

J: Something about quitting smoking. Did Harry quit smoking?

RK: He did quit smoking.

Rich: That's a verification for Randal. (ding!) Harry's way of proving that he's coming through.

J: He's also talking about vegetables. Have you changed your diet? He's saying you look great.

RK: Yes, I'm "doing vegetables" now. (Laughs.)

J: He's showing me how thin you're getting and that you don't like it so much... he's saying you need more of vitamin D or B 12...

Rich: What's more valuable for his diet Harry? Getting them naturally, or taking multi-vitamins?

J: Harry says, "That's not a good idea. He says Randal is sensitive to it (multi-vitamins)."

RK: I am.

> (Note: *Ding!* Often it's the smallest detail that helps us realize only someone on the flipside would be aware of what we do in the morning. I had no idea he was doing a veggie diet, or that he was sensitive to multi-vitamins, nor could Jennifer.)

J: Also something with your ear... He's saying you have to listen internally – you don't hear him – you smell him, he says, every once in a while.

Rich: Let's ask Harry – How can Randal hear him? Give us a one, two, three. Or let's have the class help him.

J: "You're asking him a lot," he says.

RK: They're all listening in?

J: Yeah. But the only time I listen to my dad is when I'm with Rich.

Rich: Harry, what's the best way for Randal to open his heart to hear you?

J: He says, "In the morning your drink your coffee, yes?"

RK: Yes.

J: He says you have a practice – not meditation - he's laughing. He's showing me you reading the paper or an iPad, whatever you read in the morning, when you're most open. Or late at night when you're really, really tired. You get exhausted – he just showed me a treadmill. he says over the last six months you've been better at allocating, as you normally do not allow others to do things.

RK: Yeah.

J: But the last six months it's taking the time to ask for or get help.

Yeah, I'm swamped.

He's showing me the alchemy with your body; you feel better correct?

Yeah.

He's showing me... hold on. (A loud squeaking sound from the computer) **When you drink your coffee whenever you feel open – a general term for a moment of silence, which is rare for you, get a pen and paper – he's showing me and ask him the questions and don't judge the answers... Just go with it. Bill Paxton is jumping in... "and ask him where it's coming from?" Why is Bill showing me that?**

I know Bill... I met him a few times.

Rich: Let's ask Bill what it was like to meet Randal.

J: He says he admired you – he felt goofy, he's showing me that shy Texas boy that he's so not.

Rich: I have a couple of hours of conversation with Bill, where he talks about Jim Cameron, thanks him... Jennifer didn't know who he was until Bill showed her the Titanic.

RK: Wow.

Rich: The point is Randal, you just had a wonderful conversation with someone that you knew and loved, and only you would have the feeling that he was responding to your questions.

J: I keep getting you were so loved by Harry, that you kept him on the right track. That he was a lot to handle from what I'm getting but you liked it. It was nothing you thought you couldn't handle. But he gave you a wild ride. But I feel there was no resentment, incredible sense of love and respect... and I don't get that very often when it comes to people who split up in life. I'm getting that he chose how to leave the planet.

Rich: Is that correct Randal? (Ding!)

RK: Yes, it's correct.

J: He wasn't feeling well, he had a hard time loving himself, a great front, but a very hard time loving himself. It goes back to being a little kid – he wanted it (love) so much, he didn't know how to handle it... but he wanted it from you... does that make sense?

RK: Yeah.

J: I have a question for him. I asked him "What would you have changed?" He said, "He would have changed how he felt about himself, about who he was. He could never be himself." Does that make sense?

Rich: I do in my own way.

J: It's like what the other Harry said – Harry Dean Stanton – "Don't waste time trying to worry about something you don't know." In another day and age he said he would have been a rock star.

Rich: So what are you doing now Harry?

J: He's showing me Australia... He's writing how it's going to make it better for him next time.

RK: Working out his next lifetime – like a play?

J: He's showing me that lifetime will be infused with Randal's.

Rich: So you guys are going to connect in Australia?

J: Something like that.

Rich: Harry, are you talking about the next life or some future life?

J: They're always together. He's saying, "There's always a time when he's a pain in the ass."

Rich: Wow, very cool, thanks everybody.

RK: This is really eye opening, thank you so much.

Rich: Anything you want to ask?

RK: How's he getting along with his mother?

J: He laughs and pulls his chin... hmm. "She apologized." She wasn't very kind (to him) when he was here – but she also didn't know that he kept her from a lot of things.

RK: Uh-huh.

J: Not that he's giving excuses for her behavior here, but he had a lot of guilt when she left.

RK: He left before she did.

J: Did she die two years after?

I think so.

April or something like that. He was there for her when she crossed over.

Rich: Let me ask; Harry, is it true that you asked your mother to play this role of the difficult mom for this lifetime?

J: He said, "Hell no!" Then he said, "Not consciously." Of course, he did... but he had no idea it was going to be that tough. He feels like he left the planet because he couldn't love himself.

Rich: But he sees that now, right? Harry was an artist, wasn't he?

RK: Yes.

J: He tried to create things, to bring things to life that people cannot see. If you don't have emotions, you don't learn very much. But if you have extremes, it creates something so fierce, it has to manifest itself in your art; that's what happened to him.

RK: Wow.

J: He said "Change the picture" you have of him in your house. He says, "You look good, but he doesn't." He says there's a picture of you, he actually likes the picture, you

guys are wearing jeans... he's showing the back of you guys but it's the essence of the photo he loves.

RK: I'm not aware of that photo, but I'll think about that.

J: We love you.

RK: Looking forward to seeing you again soon.

Rich: 10-4.

****

After the session, I film Jennifer looking at Randal Kleiser biography online.

What was his last name? Kleiser. Okay... he's a film director... What? Oh my gosh! "Summer Lovers?" "Blue Lagoon?" "Honey I blew up the kids?" No way. He did not direct "Grease!"

Rich: Actually, he did. The most successful musical film of all time.

Shut up. Oh my god. That's why I was getting music the whole time! That is crazy! That is so funny to me.

The best way for you to explore this journey.

If you had told it would have screw me up – the sweetest part was that Christmas movie...

Harry and Luana and I knew each other because we would be in the background when Randal was in the limelight –we used to joke about it. Harry took his own life when he realized he wouldn't survive.

That's what he said. It was his choice.

Randal made a wonderful film about it; "It's My Party."

****

Jennifer knew nothing about Harry, I knew very little about Harry, but Randal knew the most. Only he can really verify whether he felt it was accurate or not – I would guess that Randal was on the fence about whether or not Harry really did come by for a visit. There are some details that neither I nor Jennifer could have known that Harry seemed to know.

Harry Stein, from Randal Kleiser's scout while prepping "It's My Party." A photo in his home.

CHAPTER FIFTEEN:

JENNIFER'S XMAS PARTY

"Existential happiness"

Luana's Self Portrait; Richard Alcala (photo Carrie White)

Years before I met Luana, she had a boyfriend who was a famous hairdresser in Beverly Hills. Luana was by nature a shy person, so for her to be on the arm of this flamboyant Latino was something out of the ordinary for her.

She introduced him to all of her close friends, and he was one of those guys who didn't let her out of his sight when he was with her, jealous if other men looked at her – and generally embodied the "Latin lover;" something her previous boyfriends had not been.

And then one day she learned that he was sleeping with "many, if not all of his clients." He was a hairdresser who did the hair of famous women around town, and his easy access into their lives, gave him access to their bedrooms.

I'm not sure how she discovered this betrayal, but I know her reaction to it. She showed up at her friend from "acting class" Robert Towne's rental house and moved into his living room. (Luana was in Jeff Corey's acting class that included her pals Sally Kellerman, Jack Nicholson and Robert Towne.) She pulled down the curtains and didn't emerge from that room "for a month."

Robert told me the story years later, and she confirmed it as well. Imagine a month in darkness... as if that would make the pain go away. She obviously felt things very strongly, and did not forgive easily. Robert was so moved by her reaction to this betrayal, he wrote a film about it; "Shampoo" starring Warren Beatty as the hairdresser, and Luana with a small role as the receptionist of the Beverly Hills salon.

Warren Beatty asked Beverly Hills hairdresser Gene Shacove to give him advice about the profession and in all the publicity and credits, Gene was thought of as the person the film was based on. Very few knew that it was another hairdresser at the same salon "Richard Alcala" that had that distinction. (Richard was a famous hairdresser in his own right, did hair for Natalie Wood and others, went on to marry former Playmate Carrie Enwright White and had two children. Carrie writes about him in her autobiography "Upper Cut.")[50]

---

[50] https://www.imdb.com/name/nm0924584/bio

In the 1980's, Luana and I ran into Richard at an event at the Beverly Hills hotel. He was coming down the steps, his shirt open to his waist, and there were two girls with him, one on each arm. I had never met him before, Luana introduced us, and we both chuckled about it later. He was still a rake, even late in life. As his wife Carrie wrote about him in her autobiography, "He was Latin with well-cut jet-black hair, caramel tan skin, and black eyes. He had effortless cool and he smelled good. I couldn't take my teenage eyes off (him).")

When Luana heard through friends that Richard had cancer, she went to visit him often at the UCLA hospital. She helped escort him into the flipside in 1988.

She painted a painting of Richard – it was an eerie portrait that included both Luana and Richard in the frame – and nearly shared an eye on canvas. Almost like they were half and half, or two sides of the same whole.

One day, my future wife Sherry was looking at the odd portrait and thought "I wonder who is in that painting with Luana?" A few minutes later, she went for a walk on the beach, and ran into an older gentleman who introduced himself to her. *"I'm Gene Shacove."* (What are the odds?) He told her about his life, mentioned being the person the film "Shampoo" was based on – and Sherry mentioned Luana's name.

Gene said he not only knew who she was talking about, but knew the man in the painting; *"That's got to be Richard Alacala."* I looked long and hard to find a photo of Richard, and discovered one in and article about Carrie White.[51]

---

[51] https://www.huffingtonpost.com/2012/08/08/carrie-white-hair_n_1730835.html?ncid=engmodushpmg00000004

Recognized him instantly as the fellow I'd met once before on a staircase, but also as the fellow in the painting (above.)

*****

Rich: Hi class. Jennifer and I were talking about how people can do this on their own, the difference is that most people...

Jennifer: ...(interrupts) **Don't believe in it. But you are able to discern the difference between a feeling and a message. By doing so, it takes the fear out of it. If you're experiencing fear, on any level, it overrules anything that comes through. When people have emotional attachments to a situation, they're not going to get a clear message – because they'll want to hear a message.**

So that's how you're able to tell between a message and a feeling?

Yes, the question is "How do you tap in?" **We've been working with the matrix, asking questions from the other side that is invaluable information.**

First; thanks to the class for showing up. I wanted to ask about a vivid dream I had where someone I know briefly showed up to have a conversation with me. I'm fairly certain this person has no idea I had this dream, but the dream itself felt as if we were having a conversation.

Jennifer: It's a different frequency of being able to discern if you were talking to someone or their higher self... I was given an example of my friend whose husband has died, but she says, "After working on it, she gets to kiss her husband every night."

Rich: How is it that we can have a vivid dream about someone and realize they won't be able to remember the dream as we do? I was showing the Oracle of Tibet around LA, Kutenla and he asked me to come to Disneyland with him. I begged off because I was exhausted, and said "I'm sure you'll have a great time."

That night, I had a vivid dream that he knocked at my door and I let him in. He was shimmering with energy and said, "I really wish you'd come with me tomorrow." I said "Well, if you're going to go to all this trouble, okay!" The next thing I knew, the phone was ringing with his attendant saying he thought Kutenla left his camera bag in my car, and if I could bring it to him in Anaheim. I said, "Tell him I got his message, I'm on my way." Over lunch at Disneyland, I asked him if he was aware of this vivid dream I had – he was not.

They just showed me dropping bread crumbs... **from what I'm getting it's another way of giving you access to anybody that's alive.** Was the dream you had last night movie related?

Yes.

Was it Angelina Jolie?

(Pause) (ding!) Yes.

> (Note: I worked on her film "Salt." I built a website for the actors to use on set with all the film's research, and Director Phillip Noyce had me retrieve her notes each day. She is incredibly prepared, ridiculously funny, and a wise old soul. I'm not sure she'd recognize me if I was standing in front of her, but she's never appeared in any of my dreams before.)

The reason I didn't say her name is obvious. I have no idea why she appeared in the dream, but it had to be her higher self. She even made a joke about being more relaxed that herself "down here.")

I feel that she's having some issues with the strength in her hands. I can feel that.

I don't know, but I did ask questions like "So you're talking to me – but the Angie that's here on the Earth is not aware of this, is she?" What I got was her telling me "She's not aware of a lot of things, but that's okay."

(Note: People have dreams about "celebrities" all the time. The point is; either it's "made up," "some kind of metaphor," or "it is their higher self." In this case, I have no clue what the real answer is except for the unusual aspects that I remember. *"She's not aware of a lot of things"* echoes what Harry Dean Stanton said about our mutual, very much alive friend Fred Roos. "He's much more relaxed up here." Not a detail that Jennifer could have known, but accurate in terms of the Fred who is still here on the planet. *"Uptight"* isn't the right word, but "taciturn" and "doesn't suffer fools lightly" would be accurate.)

Jennifer: What I feel is happening is that by talking to her that way, it's building up for something later – it might not be conscious now, but it will be later. Now *it's so quick* – the matrix is *quickening*. (Note: During one between life session with Scott De Tamble, his client said, "Over here we call this change in consciousness "The quickening.") Even when I'm in the shower, these thoughts pop in and I always discover

292

later that it was someone texting me, talking about me, whatever. It's connected.

What's the class up to?

They're having a Christmas holiday party. They're all dancing.

Anyone wearing Santa hats?

Prince. And then Robin Williams in a Santa hat.

Ho ho ho. What's happening back there? Merry Christmas, Happy New Year.

***Happy Hanukkah.* They showed the essence of people celebrating here and how it flows up.** Pretty cool. **So when people are happy here, up there they can feel that existential happiness over there.**

It goes back and forth like a transference?

It's the heart.

You figure if people are celebrating and they think of grandpa over the holidays then grandpa is with them?

That's what holidays do for them, they can feel that energy that comes up.

Anyone see the film "Coco" up there? The Pixar film? You should see it Jennifer – it's a wonderful afterlife film. What's going on guys? Lu? what's going on? She used to do these hilarious Christmas cards.

She's good with messages. For all her friends. Like the messages now too.

One of her Christmas cards was a photograph with the caption "Merry Xmas from 32 across." They'd used her name in a...

Crossword puzzle.

That's correct. Luana, what about you and your mom, Marina? You spend time with her?

"Yes." She showed me her gardening – in the front... did she pass 20 years ago?

Yes, Luana passed 20 years ago, her mom roughly 40 years ago.

She showed me her at 8 years old – did she split?

Yes, her mother had to put Luana into foster care around then. They had a contentious relationship.

Let me see what's comes through. You've never talked about it before. **Luana is teasing me, says "You're always so cautious about conscious information... As if you would remember this!"** Um... it was gone (the rancor) **the second she got up there, all the emotion of all their lives came through -- what she was representing,** (what her mother) **was representing...**

Luana is saying "She was always trying to find a home, she could never find a place, never felt like she was in a home." She's showing me her cat, her cats represented home.

That's correct. She grew up in foster homes.(ding!) What about her dad?

She didn't trust her dad. I feel like her dad did something really bad – like she helped him and he gave his estate away to someone else... something he did that was deceiving.

That's accurate; he divorced Marina, her mother, when he got back from the war, and abandoned Luana completely. (ding!) She found him working in a bank years later, and would go to see him – pretending to hold it together, but would throw up on the way in.

They're dancing now.

Do you understand and appreciate your parent's journey now?

"Yeah." She was that for him he was that for her.

So what were the life lessons about your parents separating after your birth?

She said they were a cancer.

And all three of them did get cancer. Her mom and Luana fought at the dinner table, I realized it was because they both had low blood sugar. But now you're with each other – can you see that your mother's journey was to help you?

"Absolutely."

And her mother... was she able to see that as well?

Not at first. She showed me being in the middle of blueprints of a family tree – she went straight to that, had a hard time with her connections with her mom. **Luana was very hurt as a little kid, she was abused...** I want to get it right... hang on. **It helped her with everything else in her life as she had to**

create an alternate reality – she was abused, so she created herself outside of that.

> (Note: I knew Luana fairly well; knew she had been bounced around from foster home to foster home. It's what caused her intense privacy, part of her home later in life was sacrosanct and no one could enter. I suspected she might have been molester or harassed in some of those homes – she did tell me about one case where her foster parent would expose himself to her. We are the sum of our experiences, and from this flipside perspective, every bad event becomes a part of our skill using our art. Still, it's startling to hear about someone you love, even when it's coming years later from the flipside.)

Luana, you once said that as an actor, the more you imagined having cancer for a part, the easier it was to get cancer. Was your cancer a genetic thing, a sociological thing, or related to our breaking up?

It wasn't related to you. It wasn't related to her parents. Indirectly (it was) with you... as she showed me like a plan, "This is the way I'd want to die," and her death helped you with this research. You didn't cause the cancer, but you guys planned it out before you got here.

What about her old boyfriend Richard Alcala?

She showed me an old man with a cane. I'm seeing that guy, her boyfriend.

Richard Alcala?

(Jennifer asks Luana) "Is he here or there?" She said, **"He's here."** (Meaning he's passed away, which is accurate. *Ding!*) **They love each other.**

Luana, some people recover from the form of cancer you had – but did you want to recover from it?

Luana shakes her head. **"She didn't want to go the path her parents did."**

That's correct. She was horrified at what the cancer treatments did to her parents and didn't want any part of it.

I didn't know that.

It was stressful – more for her than me, but everyone who loved her, wished she would have seen traditional doctors.

She's very independent.

Traditional cancer methodology can and does work; although she didn't know any doctors who didn't treat her as a number.

"No. But then you wouldn't have gone on that path either. And that's how you got on this path."

We wouldn't be having this conversation. What about your dad Jennifer, does he want to weigh in on this?

I thought of him before you said that. It seems like it's easier to talk to him with you around.

Okay Jim, how can we keep you and your daughter together, so she knows it's you and you're hanging out?

My heart. The frequency of my heart. He showed me a ring (that he gave me) **– I carry in my purse. I carry it with me everywhere.**

The ring helps you to stay connected?

Yeah.

Anyone else who wants to say hi?

Who's that guy from "Big Love?"

Harry Dean Stanton?

Harry says, "Thank you."

For what?

"You annoyed people to get them to start thinking."

At his memorial, I met this one woman who was crying. I stopped her and asked how she was doing. She's married to the guy who directed "Lucky"- Harry's movie... and she was startled by what I was saying about him talking to us.

"You affected her the most. Now she's struggling to figure it out."

They told our friend Cis Rundle that Harry had said "Hand me the baby" on his deathbed. Harry? Can we ask you who the mother of this baby was?

Feels like she's up there with him. I got an R. Rose. Last name begins with a W. Weatherly sounds close.

This is a child you guys almost had – boy or girl?

He showed me blue.

This baby died in a miscarriage?

"Three months in. Bad termination." He always felt bad about it...

Can you converse with your child, now?

"Yeah, it's all energy."

Did you know this child from a previous lifetime?

"Yes." That's why he had that feeling of loss – he was an atheist, and felt he wasted a lot of time. Hold on, someone bumped him... feels like Fred. And then Amelia came in.

Hello Amelia. Fred is her navigator.

She says, "You're getting so close."

I found a picture of Amelia and Harpo Marx signed by Harpo just yesterday. "Honkistacally Yours."

"No coincidence."

She was so skinny...

"She hated that. She hated being skinny."

How'd she ever find a girlfriend if she was that skinny?

"The mind."

I'm working on her story.

"It has to come out," she said.

Who was your girlfriend again?

She was blonde... Dutch.

> (Note: For those who've read *"Hacking the Afterlife"* we go into detail about her girlfriend and her open marriage. No reason to go into that here, the topic

popped into my mind, and I always like to revisit details I've heard previously.)

How did you guys hook up? I know you were in bed with George and her when George's wife Dorothy Putnam walked in – was it easy or difficult to hook up?[52]

"No, not easy." It feels like over a summer, they were introduced... it was challenging for them. I'm looking to see when they were introduced, I saw Eleanor Roosevelt...– Did Eleanor know that Amelia was gay?

I'll assume so. Secret society and all. Since Eleanor has been "outed" by her love letters to her secretary.

So very secretive... and fleeting.

Amelia, when you're hanging out over there and showing up to different mediums or people; do you show up all over the place to a lot of different people?

"Multi-dimensionally, yes." I just asked her – Do you give them the same answer? She said **"Yes, but they half hear it, or don't hear it..."**

Fred Noonan, what about your death?

He was beheaded. We talked about that. (In *"Hacking the Afterlife"*)

---

[52] This event was reported by Dorothy Putnam to Elgen Long who told it to me during an interview. I recommended the filmmakers of "Amelia" purchase Elgen's book as historical evidence. (Long is a respected AE historian, his book ends where my story begins)

That was considered the "honorable death" by the Japanese military. Bullets meant suffering – the sword was how soldiers wanted to go?

"Yes."

So have you Fred run into any of the people that you've dealt with during your life?

"All of them."

And your predecessors were trying to figure this out?

He says, "Like we discussed, I have a connection with Amelia. She's talking about people over here figuring things out, all the coincidences they make regarding this..." She says, "It's about focus."

Focus on what?

I asked her, "Do you influence..." – she said, "That's not the right term but I enhance what you know, that's how I bring it to life." She's showing me different aspects of it.

Influencing those who are trying to understand her path and journey. So back to this painter you were in love with.

She showed me this painter – blonde, but had more freckles. There are artifacts in a museum in New York – city...

There's a museum with artifacts?

Artifacts in a museum that starts with the letter H.[53] Paintings by her. I'm getting 1962 something happened –

---

[53] https://en.wikipedia.org/wiki/New-York_Historical_Society

painter died, or her work was put into museums... **You know where her sister went to college, it felt like she met the artist there...**

I have to look it up. [54] *(Amelia's sister went to Radcliffe)*

George may be the one that introduced them. I think it's not only difficult for them to pin down dates and times, they have to go like this (gestures pulling taffy) **pulling out frequencies** – (over there) **they don't care.**

Right, if you try to pin it down **they** *may have it wrong.*

They're laughing.

Is that correct?

No, they don't have it wrong. As your buddy said, the one we were talking to, Harry Dean? **"Don't waste any time worrying about whether the afterlife exists."** That's a great message.

Okay, anyone else, class?

I just want to talk to my dad for a second. (Pause) I'm asking him to how not get sad about him... because today was the day I found out he had pancreatic cancer. He said **"But I'm here. I may not be flesh and bones but I'm here."** He's telling me – **"You tell me you want to be happy and I'll orchestrate an event to make you laugh. But if you don't open up, you block everything out. By opening up, that opens up everything."**

---

[54] Grace Muriel Earhart Morrissey was a graduate of Radcliffe and taught English at Medford High School and Belmont High. https://www.ninety-nines.org/grace-muriel-earhart-morrissey.htm

Jim let me ask you - can you put a feeling in Jennifer's body somewhere to let her know when you're with her?

My heart.

And can you amplify it? Give her a stronger amplification not related to sadness, so she can move those emotions aside?

He's like moving my mind aside. He just kicked it to the curb.

Jim, can you put something funny in her mind's eye that relates to you? Something that she's not aware of but by your putting the image into her mind, makes her aware that it's coming from you?

Oh my god. I just saw an image of an orange crayon. And then I remembered an event when I was a child looking for a crayon, and I walked into their bedroom in the midst of them making love and asked, "Where's my orange crayon?" I haven't thought about that in years.

Now I know what to get you for Christmas. Anything else?

"The more we celebrate, the more celebration energy they get."

Okay, thanks everyone. Thanks Luana. Thanks class.

*****

Congratulations! You're almost to the end of Part One. Why is there a Part One and a Part Two? Because when I was editing these sessions, I realized the more I left in that showed the process of how we asked questions, the clearer the answers became. I just split the book "down the middle."

In Part One we've spoken to people who claim things that are demonstrably inaccurate. We proven that neither Jennifer nor I fully understand what is being imparted to us – sometimes she misinterprets what she's seeing, sometimes I ask questions and get contrary answers to what the public record is.

So if that is what you were looking for, then by all means, **get a refund.** Return this book to whomever gave it to you, or *ask for your money back.* As we've said many times; we aren't here to offend anyone with these reports, we aren't here to change anyone's mind about what they believe.

As I've mentioned in my other books, I have been to many classrooms on the flipside, and as Luana was dying she told me she had a "recurring dream that she was in a classroom in another universe, and everyone was talking about spiritual things. She said she had never "hear the language" she was hearing, but somehow she understood what was being said."

In this case, Jennifer and I have been getting these reports consistently since we began meeting for lunch. ("So and so" just "showed up.") After awhile, I realized that we were having this giant group of people who were "showing up" and the classroom sprang from that concept. (As noted in Chapter One.)

On one hand, we are saying that "all these people that Luana knew, or friends of hers knew (Or Jennifer had met, or I had met) were "coming forward to speak with us." It's a literal who's who of the folks who've died while we were doing this research; from Harry Dean Stanton to Tom Petty to David Bowie to Michael Newton. I've spent 30 years in the film business, I've written and/or directed 8 theatrical features, I wrote music reviews for Variety for a number of years. I have had the experience of "meeting" or "reviewing" many of these people. I know how private they are, I know how stressful it is on their family members to lose their loved one – I'm pointing out that we are *just reporting here*. I've done my best to delete personal comments about a loved one, but if I missed one that people would not "want revealed" I'm deeply sorry for having done so.

As noted before, I've been filming people under deep hypnosis for a decade. I've filmed 45 sessions with people from all walks of life, all background, all religions. I expanded my research to include near death events, because science considers them events that can be studied. Jennifer came into my life, and we decided to take this detour – if she was able to "talk to the flipside" then it follows we could ask questions about their journey and see if it was similar or contrary to the research to date.

It's possible there will be folks who get different results. Perhaps find themselves fighting with demons, dark forces or evil characters. But it's not in this research, it's not what's reported, and it's never been the case in any of the cases we've examined. The liberating part of this research for me, is to learn that we are in control of our path and journey. Not someone else. No one can tell us what we should or shouldn't be doing unless they are intimately aware of all our previous lifetimes. That's a liberating thought unto itself.

But it goes back to the night Luana was dying and she "came to me" in my apartment in Santa Monica. The phone rang, someone said "Yo, it's Tony; you paged me." I said, "Sorry, I did not" and hung up the phone. When I laid back on the pillow the sky opened up. There was a roar louder than anything I've ever heard. I thought "Oh my God, this must be a massive earthquake!" But it was not.

In my mind's eye I saw I was in a tunnel, a bright light above, and the walls were glowing orange. Like I was in the midst of a volcano. The sound was so loud it was deafening, the light so bright I was blinded... but I was keenly aware that I was on some kind of platform "moving upwards." And at that moment I heard my friend's voice.

Luana. But it was her voice when she was about 20. I didn't know her back then, but I recognized the younger version of her voice, standing a few feet behind me.

She said, ***"Isn't this fucking amazing?"***

I was beside myself – the roar, the intensity of the vision, I fainted. I mean literally "blacked out." And when I came to, I was just "further along the tunnel." Near the top, I was aware of sparkles and fireworks... as if channel flipping between the old UHF to VHF on a black and white TV. I could see the bars, and one reality trying to replace the other.

I thought "Uh-oh, she's taking me with her." I said, "Lu, I don't think I'm supposed to go here with you." And bang – I fell asleep. When I woke the next day, I fully expected to hear she had passed; but she had not. We spent our last Sunday together like we did before. Me reading the paper to her, her paralyzed in bed, trying to breathe.

As time passed, I leaned forward and whispered "Nam myoho renge kyo" and saw a thin smile cross her lips. I called her "gongyo" group (SGI), asked if they could come and chant her into the afterlife? A number arrived, including her friend Mathilda Buck; chanting in her ear over and over again.

Her friends had called from across the globe, Charles Grodin, Jack Nicholson, Robert Towne, Fred Roos, Francis and Eleanor Coppola called from a satellite phone on a boat in Turkey, and I heard the most painful goodbyes I'll ever hear. About 4 pm. she turned to me, said "Ha, ha, ha" and left. Her two kitties watched her "fly around the room" in unison for five minutes. Then all the clocks in her home stopped at 4 pm.

Why am I recounting this last day in Luana's life? Because it happened. Just the way these reports happened. If you haven't tired of hearing me ask questions to Luana, or hearing the answers through Jennifer, I suggest picking up Book 2 of "Backstage Pass to the Flipside: Talking to the afterlife with Jennifer Shaffer (Part Two.) *We have more stories to tell.*

Our teacher, Luana

WORKBOOK FOR TALKING TO THE AFTERLIFE:

YOUR OMNISCIENT UNIVERSE - "Y.O.U."

A workbook on how to communicate to the other side.

Photo: Nasa

As noted in these pages, what we're hearing is that people on the other side are trying to get through to their loved ones here. They know what's going on over on the other side and would love to have a way to speak to, communicate, help heal or encourage loved ones *back on the planet.*

So we're going to do our best to synthesize the process. As Jennifer has said, "it's not my job to convince anyone there is an afterlife or that I have the ability to speak to someone over there. My job is to report honestly what I see or hear." Friends ask me if I "believe I am communicating with people no longer here" and I reply "I try to leave belief out of the equation. If the answers are consistent and the process to hear them can be reproduced, I'll let the data speak for itself."

In terms of what we've heard, this workbook is to help people to focus on the process that is most effective for them.

MORTON'S METHOD

Michael Newton was a psychologist who spent his life helping people to access the "between lives realm." As noted, he apparently has come through a number of times to give us advice. I asked him for a "one, two, three" method to communicate to loved ones.

   1. *Say their name.*

I asked Michael if we needed to say their name "aloud or in our head." He said, "It doesn't matter." I prefer to say a person's name three times, aloud because it forces me to focus on them. Plus it signs like some kind of old "spell" that people would talk about, so that's fun. *"Say my name thrice!"*

I asked if he liked my method of suggesting people take out a photograph and meditate on it. He said, "Don't use the word meditation because people associate it with having to do some kind of exercise." But take a look at a photograph, try to remember when it was taken, where it was taken, who was around when it was taken, what the photographer looked like, what time of day it was – everything that helps focus the mind on the person you're trying to reach.

   2. *Ask your questions.*

I recommend asking questions you don't know the answer to, because then you have a better chance of considering if it's *new information.* People tend to ask the simple questions of

"How are you?" or "Where are you?" I've done both, and the answers are often "I'm fine" and "I'm here next to you." Which are both technically accurate. It's a bit like calling someone on a cell phone and saying, "Where are you?" The answer might be "Where do you think I am, you called!" And "How are you?" might be answered with "How do you think I am? I'm talking to you, aren't I?"

I recommend five or ten questions that you might be curious about but have no idea what the answer might be. Like "Who greeted you when you crossed over?" "What do I look like from your perspective?" "If you could look in a mirror, what color of light would you see from your perspective?" "Can you zip anywhere at will? If so, where have you been?"

3. *When you hear the answer before you can form the question you'll know you have a connection.*

Which is pretty basic; when you start to ask a friend a question and they answer immediately then you know they have anticipated the question. Time works differently "over there," so don't be surprised if before you can get the first part of the question into your mind or out of your mouth, you've "heard" an answer.

I suggest writing down the first thing that comes to mind, whatever it is. Sometimes it's hard to not judge the answer, especially if it's counterintuitive, or something we didn't expect to hear.

Our first instinct is often to think "Well I must be making this up." Indeed, that's a possibility. But it's not entirely clear how you could know an answer prior to asking a question, especially if the answer is not something you expected.

For example, the night my father died, I felt him walk into the room where I was sleeping in the home he designed and built. I felt his presence, then literally felt his hand on my shoulder. I woke up saying "Dad!" He said, "I'm experiencing indescribable joy." It's not a term I'd ever heard him use.

He said, "I need you to write something down." At the time, I thought "I must be making this up, but if I'm not, maybe I should just have him say it, and I would remember it. I was afraid that turning on a light and searching for a pen and paper would disrupt whatever this experience was that I was having.

I said, "Just tell me, I'll remember." After a pause, he said it again "I need you to write something down." So I turned on the light, got the pen and paper and sat back, expecting that I wouldn't be able to hear him again.

His voice appeared inside my head, but as if it was about a foot to the left of my head. He said "I'm here with mama and papa, Vey and Rig. Tell your mother I'm here with Pat, Harry (and four other people). Tell her I love her very much. It's beautiful over here." He also had specific messages to each of my brothers. Finally at the end of this five minute exchange, I asked "So why are you telling me and not my other brothers?" He said simply "Because you can hear me."

The next morning I mentioned this to my mom, who didn't seem phased by it. When I asked who the six people were that he mentioned, she said "Oh, those were our friends who died in World War II."

They were not people I knew, and the information could not have come from my subconscious. I had never heard their names before, and it was his way of proving to her (and me) that indeed, he was speaking to me from the flipside.

I've had many of these kinds of experiences since then, both on my own, with other mediums and/or with the help of Jennifer. She may something that I don't know – that is *new information* – and I'm able to learn later on what that person meant by it. They want to speak with you. It's up to you to try to listen to them.

Jennifer often speaks of how anyone can do the kind of work that she's doing. In a nutshell, here's her method for developing your own skills in this area:

JENNIFER'S METHOD

This method is discussed in a chapter in Part Two about guides telling us how to reach out to them. I asked for a "one, two, three" on how to do that, and a teacher gave us the recipe.

"Just talk to us," she said. "That's all you have to do. And you hit the gateway."

I asked; "We've heard this from others and some of those with us now – can I ask you directly, what's a 1, 2, 3 best method of communicating with you on a conscious level?"

She said; "Close your eyes. That's the one. The 2 is to focus on the heart and have it go through your crown chakra.... And that's it. There are only two. Because that's going to be your focus, and once you've done that you talk and you're already there."

LUANA'S METHOD

I'm only aware of this method from hearing it via my wife Sherry. As noted, Sherry met Luana only once when she was paralyzed from her illness in her bed in Mar Vista.

Sherry recently had a dream where Luana appeared before her. Sherry said in the dream "Luana! How can you be here? You died 20 years ago!" Sherry said Luana showed her a miniature Lego Star Wars fighter. "I took this to get here." Luana laughed, holding up the tiny Lego model.

Sherry and our son had been looking at that same model, earlier in the day. Sherry asked, "But how is it that I can see you?"

Luana said "Think of 11:11. We meet at the decimals."

As mentioned previously, I interpret that to mean; "If you think of each 11 as a hallway – the way we would look in architectural blueprints – then imagine your loved one is on one side, and you are on the other. In order to communicate, we both have to "lean in" or adjust our frequency. You adjust the frequency so you can "meet in the middle" but both sides need to desire that outcome.

How do you adjust your frequency? Quiet solitude sometimes works, playing a song that your loved one liked, looking at a photograph and remembering them are all methods of recalling their "frequency." If you have a video of them, or a recording of them – that too will have some reference points for you to access.

It might be a letter they wrote, or a poem they left – or even their favorite book, favorite pillow, favorite article of clothing. Somehow, we instinctively "know" their frequency when we are around these things, and it helps to "amplify the signal." You send out your message, thought, or reminiscence in such a way to allow them to come forward and reveal whatever it is they want to show you.

Sometimes it takes a few hours, perhaps days or weeks for them to find the appropriate response. Sometimes its instantaneous. The idea is to "stay open to their reply." It doesn't mean we have to take every doorbell, phone call, song on the radio as "evidence they're trying to reach us" – but if there's a song on the radio and the thought pops into your head, "That's my loved ones favorite song; did you do that for me?" and you get a response – then the odds are that it is them.

There are some folks who fear that "demons" or "evil spirits" will show up instead. All I can say to that notion is that in all the accounts I've examined, worked with, or been privy too – none include anything of the sort. If they don't want to show up, don't want to reply, that's entirely possible as well.

Recently, I was responding to a woman on Quora who lived in Turkey. She was distraught because her husband died suddenly and had not reached out to her. She begged for some method to reach out to him. I suggested a number of modalities, and she wrote that she had "followed them to the letter but had gotten nothing." She was beside herself with grief. Finally I suggested that he *had* reached out to her – and that she was *just not revealing that he had.*

She replied that she did forget about a dream that she had just after he died. The dream was fleeting, and didn't end well – but for a few moments, he was there at the top of a hill, looking distraught.

I pointed out that dreams are an effective way for them to reach out to us, but they're also holograms – more information than we can imagine is included in them. If we can "freeze the dream" for a moment, we can access new information. I asked her to do so – freeze frame the memory of seeing her husband, to go up and take his hands in hers, to tell him that you'd like to know what happened or why.

She wrote that she tried that and did get a sensation which included a feeling of "overwhelming love." She also got the message that he "would reach out to her in the future" but right now her "emotions were too distraught for him to do so." She felt she had reached out to him and he had responded.

I have no way of knowing how accurate that was. It could have been her subconscious, wishful thinking, or indeed, that he had "spoken to her." But her demeanor changed instantly – from the depths of despair to something closer to grief.

She had adjusted her frequency, to allow for a moment that maybe he did still exist, and that maybe she could "take hold of his hands in a dream." And by doing so that allowed her to change grief to nostalgia. If we both adjust our frequencies, or energy, we can meet at the "decimals between the two elevens."

TRY HYPNOTHERAPY

Deep hypnosis is an excellent tool to access your loved ones on the flipside. I didn't believe I could be hypnotized, nor was I convinced people could "see anything" during that process. But that all changed with Paul Aurand, former President of the Newton Institute, said I could film their conference in Chicago. Put me directly on the path to this sentence.

While I was filming others doing hypnosis sessions, he suggested I try one and film it. I thought, "Well this will be one way to prove it's not accurate. I'm not trying to find a past life, I don't truly believe I've had one, and I don't think I can be hypnotized. It's a perfect way for me to prove it false." I came out of the session feeling as if the earth had shifted slightly on its axis. Everything I thought I knew had to be reexamined in the light of what I experienced.

Not everyone is meant to see their previous lifetimes, or to experience the between lives realm. I've filmed 45 sessions, many with Scott De Tamble (LightBetweenLives.com) and in all of the sessions he was able to not only take someone into a previous lifetime, but to help them explore their own between lives adventures. I consider him a virtuoso in the field.

But the Newton Institute has a searchable database for people trained by Michael Newton at their website (NewtonInstitute.org). That means there is someone not far from you, as they're across the globe now, who has learned how to direct people into the flipside, and can be a tour guide for that adventure.

I highly recommend interviewing whomever you choose, speaking directly to them, and explaining what it is you're looking to learn. I recommend practicing "speaking aloud" while doing a guided meditation. When you hear "picture yourself on a boat on a river," not only picture it but speak aloud about what you are seeing sensing or experiencing on that river.

Doing so gets you in the habit of speaking aloud – the oddest thing about these sessions. It's like having someone next to your bed whispering "And now what are you seeing?" And you must reply – otherwise the therapist will never know what you saw, and you won't have a record of it.

And that's key as well – any form of hypnotherapy should be accompanied by a recorder – either the therapist's or your own. Some therapists take notes – others use cameras, some use tape recorders. The reason to do so it because often what you think happened did not – and by reviewing the tape, you can hear yourself speaking, and while you're doing so more images come to mind. The next thing to do is write up a transcript. There's no harm in any of this. It's all about searching for the jewel.

People see their lost loved ones, and can embrace them. They can ask questions about why they had to leave, or what they are up to now. They often get a complicated, profound message about their path and journey – and almost always are only given as much as they need to hear so that they don't upset their own path or journey too much. After all, this isn't an exercise in "spoiling the ending" or telling everyone how the "play ends."

But some people get stuck in their grief and can't move forward. That's why hypnotherapy can be helpful, as they get to see a number of key details about their own path and journey and why things occurred the way that they have.

So aside from what Jennifer and I are doing – asking direct questions to people no longer on the planet to see what we can learn from them – I can recommend hypnotherapy as a tool to do the same. I've done five between life sessions – with different hypnotherapists. And each and every time I get to visit with my friend Luana.

She's not across the field, or on the other side of a room. She's standing next to me, holding my hand, laughing with me – scolding me – often telling me deep profound things that

I had no idea that she would access to. And for some reason, when she and I talk over there, **it feels like I know exactly what she's talking about.**

Think about that for a moment.

She's telling me things about math, science, how energy or frequency works, things that I have no access to in my current role on stage – but backstage, where she is, she's showing me – demonstrating to me – helping me to understand the most profound ideas. And I know myself well enough, know what my limitations are in this body and mind, to realize that "over there" I feel as if I know what she's saying – and that **it doesn't really matter if I get it over here.** It is what is is. I'm only here to report what I've experienced.

So check into it. If you can't find a Newton trained hypnotherapist, find one who understands the idea that we choose our lifetimes, or that we come here to experience the journey, and when we get "back home" we share it with our loved ones. If they understand that concept, then you've got a pretty good chance of having them escort you around to see and interact with your loved ones.

THE HOLOGRAPHIC MEMORY

"All memory is holographic."

Perhaps you remember the book by Michael Talbot "The Holographic Universe." [55] It was in his research that he observed that everything in the universe is holographic in

---

[55] https://www.goodreads.com/book/show/319014.The_Holographic_Universe

nature. An object exists in time and space, and therefore retains some memory of that time and space.

Photographs are holographic because they retain the magnetic energy of the moment they were taken. That means they retain the time and space of that event, and the people that are in it.

I've also found that memory is holographic. Any event that has ever happened to an individual is stored in their memory, and therefore is accessible. The mind has no delete key. But more importantly, that memory holds all of the information from that moment in time.

For example, when interviewing people who've had a near death event, I've found that we can access that event again in real time – either while under hypnosis, or not. The memory of the event still exists in their mind, and if they can access any part of it, they can access all of it. Holograms, if broken to pieces, retain all the information of the complete photograph. So even a tiny piece will contain all of the information of the original subject.

Jennifer and I both strongly believe that by accessing the flipside, we can help heal the planet. We can get people to see that they need to leave behind a clean campsite, if not for their children, but for their own return. We can get people to see that those who've gone before us are not some mysterious or frightening entity – but that we can ask them questions to help us on our path and journey.

As Harry Dean Stanton put it; **"You don't have to believe in an afterlife, or what religion tells you. However, you should believe in the possibility of an afterlife, so you won't waste any more time worrying about it."** If it's possible that there is an afterlife, then it is possible that everything you've seen in this book is true.

Finally, a word about truth.

One of our sessions addressed prevarication from the flipside. In an interview, Jennifer asked, "How do I know you are you really telling me this accurately?" The person replied, "We can't lie from over here." He went on to describe how anyone can mistranslate from either side, or not impart their message properly – but the act of lying isn't possible "because of the frequencies involved."

Jennifer: "When I started this work I was worried about how accurate this information was – I've given thousands over readings, I'm at over 3000 right now. What I've learned is that they may not know everything or can make a mistake presenting it, or I may make a mistake in my interpretation; but they are always truthful."

Rich: So why can't you prevaricate over there?

Jennifer: "He's showing me himself lying as he's talking; over here anyone can do that, but over there, the frequencies don't match up if you aren't truthful, so you can't communicate. It's different if you're unaware that what you're saying is untrue – but if you're consciously trying to say something you know to be *not true*, over there everyone can see that the frequencies don't match up. It shouts out that you're lying."

Rich: So everyone would know you were being untruthful?

Jennifer: Everyone.

Some will find these accounts of speaking to "the dead" or "dead celebrities" offensive. Some may find them to be manipulative. The person is "no longer here to defend their previous point of view, and by our claiming they still exist, it flies in the face of what they spent their lives claiming."

Well, this book isn't for you. I'm sorry if that's how you feel about it, but in nearly every interview we've done with people they've *insisted* we pass this information along. Either privately to their loved ones – and we both do that as best we can – but also they've insisted we "aim for the fences" with this work. It's not enough to offer that it's a possibility that life goes on, but to shout it to everyone in listening distance.

No one has said; *"Gee, I don't think you should write this book. It's too controversial."* The best maxim I've heard doing this research came from a film director on the flipside who said, **"No one comes over here wishing they held back more in their lifetime."** So in that vein, neither will we.

In Jennifer's case, I know she's helping families who've lost loved ones, I know she's helped people heal or to find out what really happened to their loved ones. And she does that work pro bono – she's helped countless law enforcement agencies, and has a network of mediums who do the same for no charge.

I had one woman come up to me during a book talk and say, **"I just wanted to look you in the eye and say, "Thank you for saving my life."** I know that there's no film project I would ever work on where someone would give me that kind of *review*. And in this research to understanding *"why we're on the planet"* I see clearly that the reason I'm on it, is to pass this information along.

Recently, I pointed out to a close friend that the loss of her husband wasn't a loss, as he was still available to her. She said **"I don't want to hear all that about being able to contact him. I'm holding onto my pain, as it's all I have of him."** Not up to me to take that from her.

As I'm fond of saying, **these reports are not belief, theory or opinion** – just reporting verbatim what we're hearing from people on the flipside. Jennifer is the conduit and sparkplug for this information, and my ability to remember details about the architecture of the afterlife, allows us to put these reports into a story line.

We're demonstrating that anyone can do the same kind of investigation. If you get no answers, try a different method. If you get some answers, then it bears further investigation. If you toss a jewel into a pond, it sends out waves; there's no knowing where they might end up.

People have gone through their caterpillar stage, have gone through their chrysalis stage, and are now into their butterfly stage. We are here to focus on the butterflies. *Enjoy the flight.*

Our professor Luana and puppy

ACKNOWLEDGEMENTS

ABOUT JENNIFER SHAFFER

With husband Fred

Jennifer M. Shaffer is a World-Renowned Evidential Intuitive Medium who is setting the standard for what she refers to as "The New Normal." Founding Member of JS Intuitive Investigations Academy and JS Investigation Alliances

Social Activism Award Winner, Best American Psychics Psychic of the Year. Guest on Monica the Medium, Dr. Drew on HLN, Below the Deck and Ricki Lake. Investigation Cases Profiled on Dr. Phil and 20/20. As Seen on Bravo, CBS, HLN on CNN, Fox and Free Form on ABC Television

Author, Speaker and Intuitive Spiritual Teacher, Vice President and Law Enforcement Case Expert for Beneficial Intelligence Syndicate. Impartial Witness Case Expert Through BIS for Law Enforcement, FBI Officials and The Intuitive Investigation Alliances and Academy. Advisory Board Member for FOHVAMP Families of Homicide Victims and Missing Persons.

Jennifer has been seen on CBS Television, HLN on CNN, FOX, Free Form on ABC and she just had an appearance on BRAVO. Her heart is with her JS Investigation Alliances where there is a collaboration of Intuitives that donate their time to families and law enforcement for unresolved homicides and missing person cases.

Jennifer's JS Intuitive Investigations Academy will serve as a platform and safe place for individuals to learn about investigations. She will be mentoring those who want to learn about their own abilities while working on investigations. Jennifer was recently asked to serve as an Advisory Board Member for FOHVAMP, an organization that helps Families of Homicide Victims and Missing Persons. Evidential Intuitive Medium Jennifer Shaffer Sees, Hears, and Feels those Spirits who have Crossed Over.

Jennifer is a "Translator of Spirit." She is a Clairvoyant Medium, Medical Intuitive, Intuitive Investigator and Profiler. Her investigation cases have recently been featured on "20/20" and "Dr. Phil," and she has also been a reoccurring guest on the "Ricki Lake" show. Jennifer is clairvoyant, clairaudient and clairsentient which means being blessed with sight, hearing and feeling from the spiritual world that both enlightens and brings comfort. Jennifer receives guidance that gives you confirmation of past events, informs you of the future, brings clarity to issues, and messages from your departed loved ones. Spirit wants to help by giving powerful insights from the other side.

She can be reached at JenniferShaffer.com

A THOUSAND THANKS

First and foremost, thanks to Jennifer. I bow to your skills as a medium, a medical intuitive, as someone who helps people heal. We've had many laughs during our sessions; there's nothing quite like hearing something profound and being able to laugh about it.

A shout out to Scott De Tamble, lightbetweenlives.com, to Michael Newton, thank you for your work and your research. Thanks to George Noory, his Coast to Coast and "Beyond Belief" crew at Gaia.com.

But most of all, a special thanks to Luana whom I met *40 years ago*! To think she would have such a profound influence on me in life and after is really wild. I appreciate her relentless patience, her ability to herd cats – the members of our class. Thanks to all those in attendance; Robin, David, Prince, Michael, Julian, John, Jim, Jimi, another Jim, George, Tom, Rance, Billy, Harry Dean, Cis, Randal, Harry, Robert, Edward, Craig, Sydney, Howard, Roger, Gene, Ray, Anthony, Kate, Uncle C, Rig, Paul T, Craig O, Billy M, Mom, Dad.

Thanks to those who've generously donated towards the research: Mary Fesler, Chris Rawls, Julie Harmeyer, Tash Govender, Diana Takata, Don Thompson, Alex Broskey, Savarna Wiley, Robert Thurman, Carin Levee, Chris Monaghan, John Wylie, Daniel Kearney, Maureen Johanson, Bill Dale, Eric Harrington, Lisa Yesse, Tamara Guion-Yagy, Lynette Hilton, John and Lucy Tibayan, Jon Burhham.

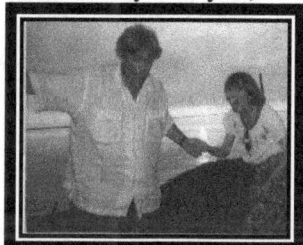

One of our last photos together

Dedicated to my wife Sherry, daughter Olivia and son RJ – I love you! *Thanks for choosing me.*

Richard Martini is a journalist, author and award-winning filmmaker. Boston University, USC Film School, Master of Professional Writing. He's written and/or directed 8 theatrical features including "You Can't Hurry Love," "Limit Up," and "Cannes Man." He wrote for Variety, Premiere and Inc.com, documentaries include "White City/Windy City – Sister Cities" "Journey Into Tibet with Robert Thurman" and "Tibetan Refugee." His books; "Flipside: A Tourist's Guide on How to Navigate the Afterlife" "It's a Wonderful Afterlife Volume 1 and 2" and "Hacking the Afterlife" are available at all online outlets. The documentary film "Flipside: A Journey Into the Afterlife" is available through Gaia TV or online. For further info: RichMartini.com

Clips and book talks can be found on www.YouTube.com/user/MartiniProds

Copyright Richard Martini 2018 © All Rights Reserved. Space photos by NASA. George Harrison Photo, Russ Titelman. All Rights Reserved.

End of book One

"Backstage Pass to the Flipside: Talking to the Afterlife with Jennifer Shaffer PART TWO" interviews:
*****
1 – "Ed Taylor, Robert & the Oscar nominated dog." Interview with Robert Towne and two friends on the flipside.
2 – "It's Fun Over Here" Interview with Oscar winning director Sydney Pollack on the flipside.
3 – "Love is a higher frequency" Producer Jonathan Krane and Marlon Brando are accessed on the flipside.
4 - "Black holes & the Infinite" Interviews with Stephen Hawking, Garry Shandling and Christopher Hitchens
5 - Jennifer and Luana "Blueprints" Actress/Teacher Luana Anders goes over how to assemble a class on the flipside.
6 - Brothers from Another Planet. Various class members weigh in on reports from the flipside.
7 - Consciousness "Unearthly Answers" More general discussions, including Bill Paxton, Tom Petty and others.
8 - John, George, Jimi "Blue Suede Shoes" Jimi Hendrix, George Harrison and John Lennon comment from the flipside.
9 – "Buddha and Jesus Walk Into a Bar." Interviews with two people who claim to be avatars.
10 - "Field Trips" An interview with Amelia Earhart and a journey to an akashic library.
11 - "Ghost Stories" Ghost Hunting with Garry Shandling, Gilda Radner and John Belushi.
12 – "Wednesday People" with Anthony Bourdain, Kate Spade and Robin Williams.
13 – "Let It Be" Afterword with Anthony Bourdain, Hal Ashby and John Lennon with some parting words.
*****

"Backstage Pass to the Flipside: Talking to the Afterlife with Jennifer Shaffer PART TWO" is available online.